No literary analysis is complete without textual evidence. Summaries, paraphrases, and quotes are all forms of textual evidence, but direct quotes from the text are the most effective form of evidence. The best textual evidence is relevant, accurate, and clearly supports the writer's claim. This can include pieces of descriptions, dialogue, or exposition that shows the applicability of the analysis to the text. Analysis that is average, or sufficient, shows an understanding of the text; contains supporting textual evidence that is relevant and accurate, if not strong; and shows a specific and clear response. Analysis that partially meets criteria also shows understanding, but the textual evidence is generalized, incomplete, only partly relevant or accurate, or connected only weakly. Inadequate analysis is vague, too general, or incorrect. It may give irrelevant or incomplete textual evidence, or may simply summarize the plot rather than analyzing the work. It is important to incorporate textual evidence from the work being analyzed and any supplemental materials and to provide appropriate attribution for these sources.

© Mometrix Media - flashcardsecrets.com/louisiana

Discuss the effective use of textual evidence when supporting a literary analysis.

Mometrix

Learn Faster. Score Higher.

At Mometrix, we think differently about tests. We believe you can perform better on your exam by implementing a few critical strategies and focusing your study time on what's most important. With so many demands on your time, you probably don't have months to spend preparing for an exam that holds the key to your future. Our team of testing experts devote hours upon hours to painstakingly review piles of content and boil it all down to the critical concepts that are most likely to be on your exam. We do a lot of work cutting through the fluff to give you what you need the most to perform well on the exam. But you don't have to take our word for it; here is what some of our customers have to say:

"This flashcard system works. It's that simple. Easy to handle, the flashcards use a proven system of giving you bite sized facts that cover all the essential concepts you need to pass the test with ease. Portable, durable and concise, these cards allow you to learn the way you learn best, through repetition. Excellent." - Joanna S.

"I have just retaken my test and I scored way better than my previous score. I had this program for only 3 days and I just want to say that I can't believe how well it worked." -Mandy C.

"These flashcards are great for both learning and studying. The questions are semi-open-ended, leaving room for a long answer, which makes them perfect for self-testing at home: I like to set up a pile of cards and answer each question on a piece of paper, finally checking my answers against the (very complete) answers printed on the backs of the cards. They're also great for quick, last-minute review: simply take them with you and use the questions to jolt your memory." - Emily M.

We offer study materials for over 1000 different standardized exams, including:

Business and Career	**Medical and Nursing**
Construction and Industry	**Teacher Certification**
Counseling and Social Work	**K-12**
Finance, Insurance, and Real Estate	**College Admissions and Placement**

For questions about bulk discounts or ordering through your company or institution, please contact our Institutional Sales Department at 888-248-1219 or sales@mometrix.com.

Visit www.MometrixCatalog.com for our full list of products and services.

Mometrix Media LLC is not affiliated with or endorsed by any official testing organization. Mometrix publishes a variety of unofficial educational materials. All organizational and test names are trademarks of their respective owners. This content is provided for test preparation purposes only and does not imply an endorsement by Mometrix of any particular political, scientific, or religious point of view.

Made in USA

In research papers, one can include studies whose conclusions agree with one's position (Reed 284; Becker and Fagen 93), as well as studies that disagree (Limbaugh 442, Beck 69) by including parenthetical citations as demonstrated in this sentence. Quotations should be selective: writers should compose an original sentence and incorporate only a few words from a research source. If students cannot use more original words than quotation, they are likely padding their compositions. However, including quotations appropriately increases the credibility of the writer and their argument.

Knowing who wrote a source and why they wrote it is important to determine whether a source is appropriate for a research project. The author should be qualified to write on the subject of the material. Their purpose may be to inform their audience of information, to present and defend an analysis, or even to criticize a work or other argument. The researcher must decide whether the author's purpose makes the source appropriate to use. The source's container and publisher are important to note because they indicate the source's reputability and whether other qualified individuals have reviewed the information in the source. Credible secondary sources should also reference other sources, primary or secondary, that support or inform the source's content. Evaluating the accuracy of the information or the presence of bias in a source will require careful reading and critical thinking on the part of the researcher. However, a source with excellent credentials may still contain pieces of inaccurate information or bias, so it is the researcher's responsibility to be careful in their use of each source.

Writers do better to include short quotations rather than long. For example, quoting six to eight long passages in a 10-page paper is excessive. It is also better to avoid wording like "This quotation shows," "As you can see from this quotation," or "It talks about." These are amateur, feeble efforts to interact with other authors' ideas. Also, writing about sources and quotations wastes words that should be used to develop one's own ideas. Quotations should be used to stimulate discussion rather than taking its place. Ending a paragraph, section, or paper with a quotation is not incorrect per se, but using it to prove a point, without including anything more in one's own words regarding the point or subject, suggests a lack of critical thinking about the topic and consideration of multiple alternatives. It can also be a tactic to dissuade readers from challenging one's propositions. Writers should include references and quotations that challenge as well as support their thesis statements. Presenting evidence on both sides of an issue makes it easier for reasonably skeptical readers to agree with a writer's viewpoint.

When using sources in a research paper, it is important to integrate information so that the flow of the composition is not interrupted as the two compositions are combined. When quoting outside sources, it is necessary to lead into the quote and ensure that the whole sentence is logical, is grammatically correct, and flows well. Below is an example of an incorrectly integrated quote.

> During the Industrial Revolution, many unions organized labor strikes "child labor, unregulated working conditions, and excessive working hours" in America.

Below is the same sentence with a properly integrated quote.

> During the Industrial Revolution, many unions organized labor strikes to protest the presence of "child labor, unregulated working conditions, and excessive working hours" in America.

In the first example, the connection between "strikes" and the quoted list is unclear. In the second example, the phrase "to protest the presence of" link the ideas together and successfully creates a suitable place for the quotation.

When quoting sources, writers should work quotations and references seamlessly into their sentences instead of interrupting the flow of their own argument to summarize a source. Summarizing others' content is often a ploy to bolster word counts. Writing that analyzes the content, evaluates it, and synthesizes material from various sources demonstrates critical thinking skills and is thus more valuable.

Three common reference styles are **MLA** (Modern Language Association), **APA** (American Psychological Association), and **Turabian** (created by author Kate Turabian, also known as the Chicago Manual of Style). Each style formats citation information differently. Professors and instructors often specify that students use one of these. Generally, APA style is used in psychology and sociology papers, and MLA style is used in English literature papers and similar scholarly projects. To understand how these styles differ, consider an imaginary article cited in each of these styles. This article is titled "Ten Things You Won't Believe Dragons Do," written by author Andra Gaines, included in the journal *Studies in Fantasy Fiction* and published by Quest for Knowledge Publishing.

MLA:
Gaines, Andra. "Ten Things You Won't Believe Dragons Do". *Studies in Fantasy Fiction*, vol. 3, no. 8, Quest for Knowledge Publishing, 21 Aug. 2019.

APA:
Gaines, A. (2019). Ten Things You Won't Believe Dragons Do. *Studies in Fantasy Fiction*, *3(8)*, 42-65.

Chicago:
Gaines, Andra. "Ten Things You Won't Believe Dragons Do," *Studies in Fantasy Fiction* 3, no. 8 (2019): 42-65.

Within each of these styles, citations, though they vary according to the type of source and how its used, generally follow a structure and format similar to those above. For example, citations for whole books will probably not include a container title or a volume number, but will otherwise look very similar.

Formal research writers must **cite all sources used**—books, articles, interviews, conversations, and anything else that contributed to the research. One reason is to **avoid plagiarism** and give others credit for their ideas. Another reason is to help readers find the sources consulted in the research and access more information about the subject for further reading and research. Additionally, citing sources helps to make a paper academically authoritative. To prepare, research writers should keep a running list of sources consulted, in an electronic file or on file cards. For every source used, the writer needs specific information. For books, a writer needs to record the author's and editor's names, book title, publication date, city, and publisher name. For articles, one needs the author's name, article title, journal (or magazine or newspaper) name, volume and issue number, publication date, and page numbers. For electronic resources, a writer will need the author's name, article information plus the URL, database name, name of the database's publisher, and the date of access.

English Conventions
© Mometrix Media - flashcardsecrets.com/louisiana
English I

Discuss qualities of credible sources and considerations for evaluating credibility.

English Conventions
© Mometrix Media - flashcardsecrets.com/louisiana
English I

Discuss considerations for effectively including quotes from sources in research papers.

English Conventions
© Mometrix Media - flashcardsecrets.com/louisiana
English I

Describe how to properly integrate quotes into research writing without disrupting the flow of the writing. Briefly discuss some reasons to avoid summarizing sources within a research paper.

English Conventions
© Mometrix Media - flashcardsecrets.com/louisiana
English I

Relate some considerations in research writing for incorporating outside sources into a paper.

English Conventions
© Mometrix Media - flashcardsecrets.com/louisiana
English I

Explain the reasons for citing sources in research papers. Identify how to prepare for writing a paper's bibliography and what information the research writer will need in order to properly cite their sources.

English Conventions
© Mometrix Media - flashcardsecrets.com/louisiana
English I

Define MLA, APA, and Turabian reference styles and describe how to create a citation in each style.

Secondary sources are sources that reference information originally provided by another source. The original source may be cited, quoted, paraphrased, or described in a secondary source. **Secondary sources** may be articles, essays, videos, or books found in periodicals, magazines, newspapers, films, databases, or websites. A secondary source can be used to reference another researcher's analysis or conclusion from a primary source. This information can inform the researcher of the existing discussions regarding their subject. These types of sources may also support the researcher's claims by providing a credible argument that contributes to the researcher's argument. Secondary sources may also highlight connections between primary sources or criticize both primary and other secondary sources. These types of secondary sources are valuable because they provide information and conclusions the researcher may not have considered or found, otherwise.

In literature review, one may examine both primary and secondary sources. Primary sources contain original information that was witnessed, gathered, or otherwise produced by the source's author. **Primary sources** can include firsthand accounts, found in sources such as books, autobiographies, transcripts, speeches, videos, photos, and personal journals or diaries. Primary sources may also include records of information, such as government documents, or personally-conducted research in sources like reports and essays. They may be found in academic books, journals and other periodicals, and authoritative databases. Using primary sources allows researchers to develop their own conclusions about the subject. Primary sources are also reliable for finding information about a person or their personal accounts and experiences. Primary sources such as photos, videos, audio recordings, transcripts, and government documents are often reliable, as they are usually objective and can be used to confirm information from other sources.

Finding sources for a research project may be intimidating or difficult. There are numerous sources available, and several research tools to help researchers find them. Starting with one of these tools can help narrow down the number of sources a researcher is working with at one time.

- **Libraries** house independent, printed publications that are organized by subject. This makes finding sources easy, since researchers can visit sections with sources relevant to their topic and immediately see what sources are available. Many libraries also offer printed journals and collections that include sources related to a common subject or written by the same author.
- **Databases** offer digital access to sources from a wide variety of libraries and online containers. To use a database, users search for keywords related to their topic or the type of source they want to use. The database then lists results related to or featuring those key words. Users can narrow their results using filters that will limit their results based on factors such as publication year, source type, or whether the sources are peer-reviewed. Database search results also list individual articles and methods of accessing the article directly. While databases help users find sources, they do not guarantee users access to each source.
- **Academic Journals** are collections of articles that cover a particular topic or fit within a certain category. These journals are often offered both online and in print. Academic journals typically contain peer-reviewed works or works that have undergone another type of reviewing process.

Textbooks are specialized materials that are designed to thoroughly instruct readers on a particular topic. Textbooks often include features such as a table of contents, visuals, an index, a glossary, headings, and practice questions and exercises.

Newspapers are collections of several written pieces and are primarily used to distribute news stories to their audience. In addition to news articles, newspapers may also include advertisements or pieces meant to entertain their audience, such as comic strips, columns, and letters from readers. Newspapers are written for a variety of audiences, as they are published on both the local and national levels.

Manuals are instructional documents that accompany a product or explain an important procedure. Manuals include a table of contents, guidelines, and instructional content. Instructional manuals often include information about safe practices, risks, and product warranty. The instructions in manuals are often presented as step-by-step instructions, as they are meant to help users properly use a product or complete a task.

Electronic texts are written documents that are read digitally and are primarily accessed online or through a network. Many electronic texts have characteristics similar to printed texts, such as a table of contents, publication information, a main text, and supplemental materials. However, electronic texts are more interactive and can be navigated more quickly. Electronic texts can also provide more accessibility, as they can be easily resized or narrated by text-to-speech software.

- The author and their purpose for writing the source
- The author's qualifications to write on the topic
- Whether the source is peer-reviewed or included in a scholarly publication
- The publisher
- The target audience
- The jargon or dialect the source is written in (e.g., academic, technical)
- The presence of bias or manipulation of information
- The date of publication
- The author's use of other sources to support their claims
- Whether any outside sources are cited appropriately in the source
- The accuracy of information presented

There are innumerable primary and secondary sources available in print and online. However, not every published or posted source is appropriate for a research project. When finding sources, the researcher must know how to evaluate each source for credibility and relevance. Not only must the sources be reliable and relevant to the research subject, but they must also be appropriate and help form an answer to the research question. As researchers progress in their research and composition, the relevance of each source will become clear. Appropriate sources will contribute valuable information and arguments to the researcher's own thoughts and conclusions, providing useful evidence to bolster the researcher's claims. The researcher has the freedom to choose which sources they reference or even change their research topic and question in response to the sources they find. However, the researcher should not use unreliable sources, and determining a source's credibility is not always easy.

English Conventions
© Mometrix Media - flashcardsecrets.com/louisiana
English I

Define primary sources. List some examples of primary sources and where they may be found. Discuss the uses and advantages of different types of primary sources.

English Conventions
© Mometrix Media - flashcardsecrets.com/louisiana
English I

Define secondary sources. Describe different types of secondary sources and how secondary sources are used in research.

English Conventions
© Mometrix Media - flashcardsecrets.com/louisiana
English I

List common sources of information and their uses.

English Conventions
© Mometrix Media - flashcardsecrets.com/louisiana
English I

List and define tools for finding sources for research writing.

English Conventions
© Mometrix Media - flashcardsecrets.com/louisiana
English I

Discuss considerations for determining a source's relevance and credibility.

English Conventions
© Mometrix Media - flashcardsecrets.com/louisiana
English I

List factors to consider when evaluating a source's credibility.

When searching published literature on a research topic, one must take thorough notes. It is common to find a reference that could be useful later in the research project, but is not needed yet. In situations like this, it is helpful to make a note of the reference so it will be easy to find later. These notes can be grouped in a word processing document, which also allows for easy compiling of links and quotes from internet research. Researchers should explore the internet regularly, view resources for their research often, learn how to use resources correctly and efficiently, experiment with resources available within the disciplines, open and examine databases, become familiar with reference desk materials, find publications with abstracts of articles and books on one's topic, use papers' references to locate the most useful journals and important authors, identify keywords for refining and narrowing database searches, and peruse library catalogues online for available sources—all while taking notes.

One of the two main parts of a literature review is searching through existing literature. The other is actually writing the review. Researchers must take care not to get lost in the information and inhibit progress toward their research goal. A good precaution is to write out the research question and keep it nearby. It is also wise to make a search plan and establish a time limit in advance. Finding a seemingly endless number of references indicates a need to revisit the research question because the topic is too broad. Finding too little material means that the research topic is too narrow. With new or cutting-edge research, one may find that nobody has investigated this particular question. This requires systematic searching, using abstracts in periodicals for an overview of available literature, research papers or other specific sources to explore its reference, and references in books and other sources.

The first step of a literature review paper is to create a rough draft. The next step is to edit: rewrite for clarity, eliminate unnecessary verbiage, and change terminology that could confuse readers. After editing, a writer should ask others to read and give feedback. Additionally, the writer should read the paper aloud to hear how it sounds, editing as needed. Throughout a literature review, the writer should not only summarize and comment on each source reviewed, but should also relate these findings to the original research question. The writer should explicitly state in the conclusion how the research question and pertinent literature interaction is developed throughout the body, reflecting on insights gained through the process.

As one searches for references, one will gradually develop an overview of the body of literature available for his or her subject. This signals the time to prepare for writing the literature review. The researcher should assemble his or her notes along with copies of all the journal articles and all the books he or she has acquired. Then one should write the research question again at the top of a page and list below it all of the author names and keywords discovered while searching. It is also helpful to observe whether any groups or pairs of these stand out. These activities are parts of structuring one's literature review—the first step for writing a thesis, dissertation, or research paper. Writers should rewrite their work as necessary rather than expecting to write only one draft. However, stopping to edit along the way can distract from the momentum of writing the first draft. If the writer is dissatisfied with a certain part of the draft, it may be better to skip to a later portion of the paper and revisit the problem section at another time.

After composing a rough draft of a research paper, the writer should **edit** it. The purpose of the paper is to communicate the answer to one's research question in an efficient and effective manner. The writing should be as **concise** and **clear** as possible, and the style should also be consistent. Editing is often easier to do after writing the first draft rather than during it, as taking time between writing and editing allows writers to be more objective. If the paper includes an abstract and an introduction, the writer should compose these after writing the rest, when he or she will have a better grasp of the theme and arguments. Not all readers understand technical terminology or long words, so writers should use these sparingly. Finally, writers should consult a writing and style guide to address any industry- or institution-specific issues that may arise as they edit.

When preparing to submit or otherwise publish research, it may be necessary to compose a summary or abstract to accompany the research composition.

A summary is a brief description of the contents of a longer work that provides an overview of the work and may include its most important details. One common type of summary is an abstract. Abstracts are specialized summaries that are most commonly used in the context of research. Abstracts may include details such as the purpose for the research, the researcher's methodology, and the most significant results of the research. Abstracts sometimes include sections and headings, where most summaries are limited to one or a few paragraphs with no special groupings.

English Conventions
© Mometrix Media - flashcardsecrets.com/louisiana
English I

Identify the two main parts of a literature review in research writing. Relate some guidelines for conducting a review of the literature on a research topic.

English Conventions
© Mometrix Media - flashcardsecrets.com/louisiana
English I

Describe some tips for conducting a review of research literature prior to writing the literature review.

English Conventions
© Mometrix Media - flashcardsecrets.com/louisiana
English I

Share some guidelines for writing a research literature review after completing the researching, reading, and preparing portions of reviewing the literature on a research topic. Briefly discuss considerations for editing the literature review.

English Conventions
© Mometrix Media - flashcardsecrets.com/louisiana
English I

Briefly discuss steps of the writing process in the context of composing a literature review. Identify specific elements that should be included in a literature review's body and conclusion.

English Conventions
© Mometrix Media - flashcardsecrets.com/louisiana
English I

Define summaries and abstracts in the context of research writing.

English Conventions
© Mometrix Media - flashcardsecrets.com/louisiana
English I

Comment on some general principles for editing and revising a research paper in progress.

Visit *mometrix.com/academy* for a related video.
Enter video code: 674181

Researchers should prepare some information before gathering sources. Researchers who have chosen a **research question** should choose key words or names that pertain to their question. They should also identify what type of information and sources they are looking for. Researchers should consider whether secondary or primary sources will be most appropriate for their research project. As researchers find credible and appropriate sources, they should be prepared to adjust the scope of their research question or topic in response to the information and insights they gather.

Thesis, Body Paragraphs, and Conclusion in Research Writing

Thesis	A brief proposal of a solution to a problem. Theses do not include their own support, but are supported by later evidence.
Body Paragraphs	Paragraphs focused on the primary supporting evidence for the main idea of the thesis. There are usually three body paragraphs, but there can be more if needed.
Conclusion	A final wrap-up of the research project. The conclusion should reiterate the problem, question, thesis, and briefly mention how the main evidences support the thesis.

Synthesizing information requires the researcher to integrate sources and their own thoughts by quoting, paraphrasing, or summarizing outside information in their research project. Synthesizing information indicates that the research complements the writer's claims, ensures that the ideas in the composition flow logically, and makes including small details and quotes easier. Paraphrasing is one of the simplest ways to integrate a source. **Paraphrasing** allows the writer to support their ideas with research while presenting the information in their own words, rather than using the source's original wording. Paraphrasing also allows the writer to reference the source's main ideas instead of specific details. While paraphrasing does not require the writer to quote the source, it still entails a direct reference to the source, meaning that any paraphrased material still requires a citation.

As researchers find potential sources for their research project, it is important to keep a **record** of the material they find and note how each source may impact their work. When taking these notes, researchers should keep their research question or outline in mind and consider how their chosen references would complement their discussion. **Literature reviews** and **annotated bibliographies** are helpful tools for evaluating sources, as they require the researcher to consider the qualities and offerings of the sources they choose to use. These tools also help researchers synthesize the information they find.

Understanding what is considered to be plagiarism is important to preventing unintentional plagiarism. Using another person's work in any way without proper attribution is **plagiarism**. However, it is easy to mistakenly commit plagiarism by improperly citing a source or creating a citation that is not intended for the way the source was used. Even when an honest attempt to attribute information is made, small errors can still result in plagiarized content. For this reason, it is important to create citations carefully and review citations before submitting or publishing research. It is also possible to plagiarize one's own work. This occurs when a writer has published work with one title and purpose and then attempts to publish it again as new material under a new title or purpose.

While researchers should combine research with their own ideas, the information and ideas that come from outside sources should be attributed to the author of the source. When conducting research, it is helpful to record the publication information for each source so that **citations** can be easily added within the composition. Keeping a close record of the source of each idea in a composition or project is helpful for avoiding plagiarism, as both direct and indirect references require documentation.

English Conventions
© Mometrix Media - flashcardsecrets.com/louisiana
English I

Define thesis, body paragraphs, and conclusion as parts of research writing.

English Conventions
© Mometrix Media - flashcardsecrets.com/louisiana
English I

Describe steps researchers should take after forming a research question and considerations for seeking out sources and adjusting the research question.

English Conventions
© Mometrix Media - flashcardsecrets.com/louisiana
English I

Describe helpful tools and methods for collecting information and sources for research writing.

English Conventions
© Mometrix Media - flashcardsecrets.com/louisiana
English I

Discuss synthesizing information. Define paraphrasing and describe it as a method of synthesizing information.

English Conventions
© Mometrix Media - flashcardsecrets.com/louisiana
English I

Discuss using outside sources and considerations for citing sources and avoiding plagiarism.

English Conventions
© Mometrix Media - flashcardsecrets.com/louisiana
English I

Define plagiarism and discuss considerations for avoiding different forms of plagiarism.

Resumes are brief, but formal, documents that outline an individual's experience in a certain area. Resumes are most often used for job applications. Such resumes will list the applicant's work experience, certification, and achievements or qualifications related to the position. Resumes should only include the most pertinent information. They should also use strategic formatting to highlight the applicant's most impressive experiences and achievements, to ensure the document can be read quickly and easily, and to eliminate both visual clutter and excessive negative space.

Editorials are articles in newspapers, magazines, and other serial publications. Editorials express an opinion or belief belonging to the majority of the publication's leadership. This opinion or belief generally refers to a specific issue, topic, or event. These articles are authored by a member, or a small number of members, of the publication's leadership and are often written to affect their readers, such as persuading them to adopt a stance or take a particular action.

A memorandum, also called a memo, is a formal method of communication used in professional settings. Memoranda are printed documents that include a heading listing the sender and their job title, the recipient and their job title, the date, and a specific subject line. Memoranda often include an introductory section explaining the reason and context for the memorandum. Next, a memorandum includes a section with details relevant to the topic. Finally, the memorandum will conclude with a paragraph that politely and clearly defines the sender's expectations of the recipient.

Reports summarize the results of research, new methodology, or other developments in an academic or professional context. Reports often include details about methodology and outside influences and factors. However, a report should focus primarily on the results of the research or development. Reports are objective and deliver information efficiently, sacrificing style for clear and effective communication.

Topic, Problem Statement, Research Question, and Literature Review in Research Writing

Topic	The general idea the research is about. This is usually broader than the problem itself. Example: Clean Water
Problem Statement	A problem statement is a brief, clear description of a problem with the topic. Example: Not all villages in third-world countries have ready access to clean water.
Research Question	A research question asks a specific question about what needs to be learned or done about the problem statement. Example: What can local governments do to improve access to clean water?
Literature Review	A review of the body of literature by the researcher to show what is already known about the topic and the problem. If the literature review shows that the research question has already been thoroughly answered, the researcher should consider changing problem statements to something that has not been solved.

Writing for research is essentially writing to answer a question or a problem about a particular **research topic**. A **problem statement** is written to clearly define the problem with a topic before asking about how to solve the problem. A **research question** serves to ask what can be done to address the problem. Before a researcher should try to solve a problem, the researcher should spend significant time performing a **literature review** to find out what has already been learned about the topic and if there are already solutions in place. The literature review can help to re-evaluate the research question as well. If the question has not been thoroughly answered, then it is proper to do broader research to learn about the topic and build up the body of literature. If the literature review provides plenty of background, but no practical solutions to the problem, then the research question should be targeted at solving a problem more directly. After the research has been performed, a **thesis** can act as a proposal for a solution or as a recommendation to future researchers to continue to learn more about the topic. The thesis should then be supported by significant contributing evidence to help support the proposed solution.

English Conventions
© Mometrix Media - flashcardsecrets.com/louisiana
English I

Briefly define editorials.

English Conventions
© Mometrix Media - flashcardsecrets.com/louisiana
English I

Define resumes and identify some common standards for creating resumes.

English Conventions
© Mometrix Media - flashcardsecrets.com/louisiana
English I

Describe the use of reports in academic or professional contexts.

English Conventions
© Mometrix Media - flashcardsecrets.com/louisiana
English I

Describe a memorandum.

English Conventions
© Mometrix Media - flashcardsecrets.com/louisiana
English I

Define research topic, problem statement, and thesis as parts of research writing. Describe the steps and purpose of a literature review.

English Conventions
© Mometrix Media - flashcardsecrets.com/louisiana
English I

Define topic, problem statement, research question, and literature review as parts of research writing.

The Diary of a Young Girl by Dutch Jew Anne Frank (1947) contains her life-affirming, nonfictional diary entries from 1942-1944 while her family hid in an attic from World War II's genocidal Nazis. *Go Ask Alice* (1971) by Beatrice Sparks is a cautionary, fictional novel in the form of diary entries by Alice, an unhappy, rebellious teen who takes LSD, runs away from home and lives with hippies, and eventually returns home. Frank's writing reveals an intelligent, sensitive, insightful girl, raised by intellectual European parents—a girl who believes in the goodness of human nature despite surrounding atrocities. Alice, influenced by early 1970s counterculture, becomes less optimistic. However, similarities can be found between them: Frank dies in a Nazi concentration camp while the fictitious Alice dies from a drug overdose. Both young women are also unable to escape their surroundings. Additionally, adolescent searches for personal identity are evident in both books.

A **journal** is a personal account of events, experiences, feelings, and thoughts. Many people write journals to express their feelings and thoughts or to help them process experiences they have had. Since journals are **private documents** not meant to be shared with others, writers may not be concerned with grammar, spelling, or other mechanics. However, authors may write journals that they expect or hope to publish someday; in this case, they not only express their thoughts and feelings and process their experiences, but they also attend to their craft in writing them. Some authors compose journals to record a particular time period or a series of related events, such as a cancer diagnosis, treatment, surviving the disease, and how these experiences have changed or affected them. Other experiences someone might include in a journal are recovering from addiction, journeys of spiritual exploration and discovery, time spent in another country, or anything else someone wants to personally document. Journaling can also be therapeutic, as some people use journals to work through feelings of grief over loss or to wrestle with big decisions.

The Greek word for "letter" is *epistolē*, which became the English word "epistle." The earliest letters were called epistles, including the New Testament's epistles from the apostles to the Christians. In ancient Egypt, the writing curriculum in scribal schools included the epistolary genre. Epistolary novels frame a story in the form of letters. Examples of noteworthy epistolary novels include:

- *Pamela* (1740), by 18th-century English novelist Samuel Richardson
- *Shamela* (1741), Henry Fielding's satire of *Pamela* that mocked epistolary writing.
- *Lettres persanes* (1721) by French author Montesquieu
- *The Sorrows of Young Werther* (1774) by German author Johann Wolfgang von Goethe
- *The History of Emily Montague* (1769), the first Canadian novel, by Frances Brooke
- *Dracula* (1897) by Bram Stoker
- *Frankenstein* (1818) by Mary Shelley
- *The Color Purple* (1982) by Alice Walker

Letters are messages written to other people. In addition to letters written between individuals, some writers compose letters to the editors of newspapers, magazines, and other publications, while some write "Open Letters" to be published and read by the general public. Open letters, while intended for everyone to read, may also identify a group of people or a single person whom the letter directly addresses. In everyday use, the most-used forms are business letters and personal or friendly letters. Both kinds share common elements: business or personal letterhead stationery; the writer's return address at the top; the addressee's address next; a salutation, such as "Dear [name]" or some similar opening greeting, followed by a colon in business letters or a comma in personal letters; the body of the letter, with paragraphs as indicated; and a closing, like "Sincerely/Cordially/Best regards/etc." or "Love," in intimate personal letters.

1. Format all posts for smooth page layout and easy scanning.
2. Column width should not be too wide, as larger lines of text can be difficult to read
3. Headings and subheadings separate text visually, enable scanning or skimming, and encourage continued reading.
4. Bullet-pointed or numbered lists enable quick information location and scanning.
5. Punctuation is critical, so beginners should use shorter sentences until confident in their knowledge of punctuation rules.
6. Blog paragraphs should be far shorter—two to six sentences each—than paragraphs written on paper to enable "chunking" because reading onscreen is more difficult.
7. Sans-serif fonts are usually clearer than serif fonts, and larger font sizes are better.
8. Highlight important material and draw attention with **boldface**, but avoid overuse. Avoid hard-to-read *italics* and ALL CAPITALS.
9. Include enough blank spaces: overly busy blogs tire eyes and brains. Images not only break up text but also emphasize and enhance text and can attract initial reader attention.
10. Use background colors judiciously to avoid distracting the eye or making it difficult to read.
11. Be consistent throughout posts, since people read them in different orders.
12. Tell a story with a beginning, middle, and end.

The word "blog" is derived from "weblog" and refers to writing done exclusively on the internet. Readers of reputable newspapers expect quality content and layouts that enable easy reading. These expectations also apply to blogs. For example, readers can easily move visually from line to line when columns are narrow, while overly wide columns cause readers to lose their places. Blogs must also be posted with layouts enabling online readers to follow them easily. However, because the way people read on computer, tablet, and smartphone screens differs from how they read print on paper, formatting and writing blog content is more complex than writing newspaper articles. Two major principles are the bases for blog-writing rules: The first is while readers of print articles skim to estimate their length, online they must scroll down to scan; therefore, blog layouts need more subheadings, graphics, and other indications of what information follows. The second is onscreen reading can be harder on the eyes than reading printed paper, so legibility is crucial in blogs.

English Conventions
© Mometrix Media - flashcardsecrets.com/louisiana
English I

Describe journals and discuss their various uses.

English Conventions
© Mometrix Media - flashcardsecrets.com/louisiana
English I

Compare and contrast two books written in diary form, both by 20th-century teenage girls, one nonfictional and one fictional.

Visit *mometrix.com/academy* for a related video.
Enter video code: 432845

English Conventions
© Mometrix Media - flashcardsecrets.com/louisiana
English I

Describe letters as a writing form. Identify different types of letters for everyday use.

English Conventions
© Mometrix Media - flashcardsecrets.com/louisiana
English I

Identify some examples in literature wherein authors use the letter form of writing.

English Conventions
© Mometrix Media - flashcardsecrets.com/louisiana
English I

Define a blog, describe some similarities and differences between blog-writing rules and print journalism rules, and identify two major principles on which blog-writing rules are based.

English Conventions
© Mometrix Media - flashcardsecrets.com/louisiana
English I

Summarize some rules and rationales for writing blogs to make them easier to read, and to encourage readers to continue reading an entire blog post.

A writer's choice of words is a signature of their style. Careful thought about the use of words can improve a piece of writing. A passage can be an exciting piece to read when attention is given to the use of vivid or specific nouns rather than general ones.

Example:
General: His kindness will never be forgotten.
Specific: His thoughtful gifts and bear hugs will never be forgotten.

Attention should also be given to the kind of verbs that are used in sentences. Active verbs (e.g., run, swim) are about an action. Whenever possible, an **active verb should replace a linking verb** to provide clear examples for arguments and to strengthen a passage overall. When using an active verb, one should be sure that the verb is used in the active voice instead of the passive voice. Verbs are in the active voice when the subject is the one doing the action. A verb is in the passive voice when the subject is the recipient of an action.

Example:
Passive: The winners were called to the stage by the judges.
Active: The judges called the winners to the stage.

Tone may be defined as the writer's **attitude** toward the topic, and to the audience. This attitude is reflected in the language used in the writing. The tone of a work should be **appropriate to the topic** and to the intended audience. While it may be fine to use slang or jargon in some pieces, other texts should not contain such terms. Tone can range from humorous to serious and any level in between. It may be more or less formal, depending on the purpose of the writing and its intended audience. All these nuances in tone can flavor the entire writing and should be kept in mind as the work evolves.

When preparing to write a composition, consider the audience and purpose to choose the best type of writing. Four common types of writing are persuasive, expository, and narrative. **Persuasive**, or argumentative writing, is used to convince the audience to take action or agree with the author's claims. **Expository** writing is meant to inform the audience of the author's observations or research on a topic. **Narrative** writing is used to tell the audience a story and often allows more room for creativity. **Descriptive** writing is when a writer provides a substantial amount of detail to the reader so he or she can visualize the topic. While task, purpose, and audience inform a writer's mode of writing, these factors also impact elements such as tone, vocabulary, and formality.

For example, students who are writing to persuade their parents to grant them some additional privilege, such as permission for a more independent activity, should use more sophisticated vocabulary and diction that sounds more mature and serious to appeal to the parental audience. However, students who are writing for younger children should use simpler vocabulary and sentence structure, as well as choose words that are more vivid and entertaining. They should treat their topics more lightly, and include humor when appropriate. Students who are writing for their classmates may use language that is more informal, as well as age-appropriate.

Conciseness is writing that communicates a message in the fewest words possible. Writing concisely is valuable because short, uncluttered messages allow the reader to understand the author's message more easily and efficiently. Planning is important in writing concise messages. If you have in mind what you need to write beforehand, it will be easier to make a message short and to the point. Do not state the obvious.

Revising is also important. After the message is written, make sure you have effective, pithy sentences that efficiently get your point across. When reviewing the information, imagine a conversation taking place, and concise writing will likely result.

A less common type of essay is the reflective essay. **Reflective essays** allow the author to reflect, or think back, on an experience and analyze what they recall. They should consider what they learned from the experience, what they could have done differently, what would have helped them during the experience, or anything else that they have realized from looking back on the experience. Reflection essays incorporate both objective reflection on one's own actions and subjective explanation of thoughts and feelings. These essays can be written for a number of experiences in a formal or informal context.

Autobiographical narratives are narratives written by an author about an event or period in their life. Autobiographical narratives are written from one person's perspective, in first person, and often include the author's thoughts and feelings alongside their description of the event or period. Structure, style, or theme varies between different autobiographical narratives, since each narrative is personal and specific to its author and his or her experience.

English Conventions
© Mometrix Media - flashcardsecrets.com/louisiana
English I

Explain why tone is important in writing.

Visit *mometrix.com/academy* for a related video.
Enter video code: 416961

English Conventions
© Mometrix Media - flashcardsecrets.com/louisiana
English I

Discuss the importance of word choice, particularly in regard to verbs and voice.

Visit *mometrix.com/academy* for a related video.
Enter video code: 197863

English Conventions
© Mometrix Media - flashcardsecrets.com/louisiana
English I

Discuss the need for conciseness in your writing.

English Conventions
© Mometrix Media - flashcardsecrets.com/louisiana
English I

Discuss how an author's target audience influences various aspects of their writing and give examples of adaptations an author should make for different audiences.

Visit *mometrix.com/academy* for related videos.
Enter video codes: 146627 and 511819

English Conventions
© Mometrix Media - flashcardsecrets.com/louisiana
English I

Describe autobiographical narratives.

English Conventions
© Mometrix Media - flashcardsecrets.com/louisiana
English I

Describe reflective essays.

Clichés are phrases that have been **overused** to the point that the phrase has no importance or has lost the original meaning. These phrases have no originality and add very little to a passage. Therefore, most writers will avoid the use of clichés. Another option is to make changes to a cliché so that it is not predictable and empty of meaning.

Examples:
> When life gives you lemons, make lemonade.
> Every cloud has a silver lining.

The relationship between writer and reader is important in choosing a **level of formality** as most writing requires some degree of formality. **Formal writing** is for addressing a superior in a school or work environment. Business letters, textbooks, and newspapers use a moderate to high level of formality. **Informal writing** is appropriate for private letters, personal emails, and business correspondence between close associates.

For your exam, you will want to be aware of informal and formal writing. One way that this can be accomplished is to watch for shifts in point of view in the essay. For example, unless writers are using a personal example, they will rarely refer to themselves (e.g., "*I* think that *my* point is very clear.") to avoid being informal when they need to be formal.

Also, be mindful of an author who addresses his or her audience **directly** in their writing (e.g., "Readers, *like you*, will understand this argument.") as this can be a sign of informal writing. Good writers understand the need to be consistent with their level of formality. Shifts in levels of formality or point of view can confuse readers and cause them to discount the message.

Slang is an **informal** and sometimes private language that is understood by some individuals. Slang terms have some usefulness, but they can have a small audience. So, most formal writing will not include this kind of language.

Examples:
> "Yes, the event was a blast!" (In this sentence, *blast* means that the event was a great experience.)
> "That attempt was an epic fail." (By *epic fail*, the speaker means that his or her attempt was not a success.)

Jargon is **specialized vocabulary** that is used among members of a certain trade or profession. Since jargon is understood by only a small audience, writers will use jargon in passages that will only be read by a specialized audience. For example, medical jargon should be used in a medical journal but not in a New York Times article. Jargon includes exaggerated language that tries to impress rather than inform. Sentences filled with jargon are not precise and are difficult to understand.

Examples:
> "He is going to *toenail* these frames for us." (Toenail is construction jargon for nailing at an angle.)
> "They brought in a *kip* of material today." (Kip refers to 1000 pounds in architecture and engineering.)

In educational settings, students are often expected to use academic language in their schoolwork. Academic language is also commonly found in dissertations and theses, texts published by academic journals, and other forms of academic research. Academic language conventions may vary between fields, but general academic language is free of slang, regional terminology, and noticeable grammatical errors. Specific terms may also be used in academic language, and it is important to understand their proper usage. A writer's command of academic language impacts their ability to communicate in an academic or professional context. While it is acceptable to use colloquialisms, slang, improper grammar, or other forms of informal speech in social settings or at home, it is inappropriate to practice non-academic language in academic contexts.

A colloquialism is a word or phrase that is found in informal writing. Unlike slang, **colloquial language** will be familiar to a greater range of people. However, colloquialisms are still considered inappropriate for formal writing. Colloquial language can include some slang, but these are limited to contractions for the most part.

Examples:
> "Can *y'all* come back another time?" (Y'all is a contraction of "you all.")
> "Will you stop him from building this *castle in the air*?" (A "castle in the air" is an improbable or unlikely event.)

English Conventions
© Mometrix Media - flashcardsecrets.com/louisiana
English I

Discuss the relationship between writer and reader.

English Conventions
© Mometrix Media - flashcardsecrets.com/louisiana
English I

Define and discuss clichés.

English Conventions
© Mometrix Media - flashcardsecrets.com/louisiana
English I

Define and discuss the use of jargon.

English Conventions
© Mometrix Media - flashcardsecrets.com/louisiana
English I

Discuss the use of slang.

English Conventions
© Mometrix Media - flashcardsecrets.com/louisiana
English I

Define and discuss the use of colloquialisms.

English Conventions
© Mometrix Media - flashcardsecrets.com/louisiana
English I

Define academic language and discuss its use and importance.

Transitions between sentences and paragraphs guide readers from idea to idea and indicate relationships between sentences and paragraphs. Writers should be judicious in their use of transitions, inserting them sparingly. They should also be selected to fit the author's purpose—transitions can indicate time, comparison, and conclusion, among other purposes. Tone is also important to consider when using transitional phrases, varying the tone for different audiences. For example, in a scholarly essay, *in summary* would be preferable to the more informal *in short*.

When working with transitional words and phrases, writers usually find a natural flow that indicates when a transition is needed. In reading a draft of the text, it should become apparent where the flow is disrupted. At this point, the writer can add transitional elements during the revision process. Revising can also afford an opportunity to delete transitional devices that seem heavy handed or unnecessary.

When a paragraph opens with the topic sentence, the second sentence may begin with a phrase like *first of all*, introducing the first supporting detail or example. The writer may introduce the second supporting item with words or phrases like *also*, *in addition*, and *besides*. The writer might introduce succeeding pieces of support with wording like, *another thing*, *moreover*, *furthermore*, or *not only that, but*. The writer may introduce the last piece of support with *lastly*, *finally*, or *last but not least*. Writers get off the point by presenting off-target items not supporting the main point. For example, a main point *my dog is not smart* is supported by the statement, *he's six years old and still doesn't answer to his name*. But *he cries when I leave for school* is not supportive, as it does not indicate lack of intelligence. Writers stay on point by presenting only supportive statements that are directly relevant to and illustrative of their main point.

Transitional Words and Phrases

Examples	for example, for instance, such as, to illustrate, indeed, in fact, specifically
Place	near, far, here, there, to the left/right, next to, above, below, beyond, opposite, beside
Concession	granted that, naturally, of course, it may appear, although it is true that
Repetition, Summary, or Conclusion	as mentioned earlier, as noted, in other words, in short, on the whole, to summarize, therefore, as a result, to conclude, in conclusion
Addition	and, also, furthermore, moreover
Generalization	in broad terms, broadly speaking, in general

Transitional Words and Phrases

Time	Afterward, immediately, earlier, meanwhile, recently, lately, now, since, soon, when, then, until, before, etc.
Sequence	too, first, second, further, moreover, also, again, and, next, still, besides, finally
Comparison	similarly, in the same way, likewise, also, again, once more
Contrasting	but, although, despite, however, instead, nevertheless, on the one hand... on the other hand, regardless, yet, in contrast.
Cause and Effect	because, consequently, thus, therefore, then, to this end, since, so, as a result, if... then, accordingly

Linguistic form encodes the literal meanings of words and sentences. It comes from the phonological, morphological, syntactic, and semantic parts of a language. **Writing style** consists of different ways of encoding the meaning and indicating figurative and stylistic meanings. An author's writing style can also be referred to as his or her **voice**.

Writers' stylistic choices accomplish three basic effects on their audiences:
- They **communicate meanings** beyond linguistically dictated meanings,
- They communicate the **author's attitude**, such as persuasive or argumentative effects accomplished through style, and
- They communicate or **express feelings**.

Within style, component areas include: narrative structure; viewpoint; focus; sound patterns: meter and rhythm; lexical and syntactic repetition and parallelism; writing genre; representational, realistic, and mimetic effects; representation of thought and speech; meta-representation (representing representation); irony; metaphor and other indirect meanings; representation and use of historical and dialectal variations; gender-specific and other group-specific speech styles, both real and fictitious; and analysis of the processes for inferring meaning from writing.

Two important principles to consider when writing a conclusion are strength and closure. A strong conclusion gives the reader a sense that the author's main points are meaningful and important, and that the supporting facts and arguments are convincing, solid, and well developed. When a conclusion achieves closure, it gives the impression that the writer has stated all necessary information and points and completed the work, rather than simply stopping after a specified length. Some things to avoid when writing concluding paragraphs include:
- Introducing a completely new idea
- Beginning with obvious or unoriginal phrases like "In conclusion" or "To summarize"
- Apologizing for one's opinions or writing
- Repeating the thesis word for word rather than rephrasing it
- Believing that the conclusion must always summarize the piece

English Conventions
© Mometrix Media - flashcardsecrets.com/louisiana
English I

Give some examples of specific words in a piece of writing that signal the introduction of successive details supporting the main point. Explain, using examples, how writers can stray away from or stay on the point.

English Conventions
© Mometrix Media - flashcardsecrets.com/louisiana
English I

Explain transitions in depth.

Visit *mometrix.com/academy* for a related video.
Enter video code: 233246

English Conventions
© Mometrix Media - flashcardsecrets.com/louisiana
English I

Give some examples of transitional words and phrases related to time, sequence, comparison and contrast, and cause and effect.

English Conventions
© Mometrix Media - flashcardsecrets.com/louisiana
English I

Give some examples of transitional words and phrases related to examples, place, concession, repetition, summary, conclusion, addition, and generalization.

Visit *mometrix.com/academy* for a related video.
Enter video code: 707563

English Conventions
© Mometrix Media - flashcardsecrets.com/louisiana
English I

Identify two important principles for writing the conclusion of an essay or composition and briefly explain each. Identify some writing pitfalls to avoid when composing a concluding paragraph.

Visit *mometrix.com/academy* for a related video.
Enter video code: 209408

English Conventions
© Mometrix Media - flashcardsecrets.com/louisiana
English I

Define how writing style differs from linguistic form. Identify three effects that stylistic choices have upon reading and listening audiences. Identify some component areas within style.

Common methods of adding substance to paragraphs include examples, illustrations, analogies, and cause and effect.

- **Examples** are supporting details to the main idea of a paragraph or a passage. When authors write about something that their audience may not understand, they can provide an example to show their point. When authors write about something that is not easily accepted, they can give examples to prove their point.
- **Illustrations** are extended examples that require several sentences. Well-selected illustrations can be a great way for authors to develop a point that may not be familiar to their audience.
- **Analogies** make comparisons between items that appear to have nothing in common. Analogies are employed by writers to provoke fresh thoughts about a subject. These comparisons may be used to explain the unfamiliar, to clarify an abstract point, or to argue a point. Although analogies are effective literary devices, they should be used carefully in arguments. Two things may be alike in some respects but completely different in others.
- **Cause and effect** is an excellent device to explain the connection between an action or situation and a particular result. One way that authors can use cause and effect is to state the effect in the topic sentence of a paragraph and add the causes in the body of the paragraph. This method can give an author's paragraphs structure, which always strengthens writing.

For most forms of writing, you will need to use multiple paragraphs. As such, determining when to start a new paragraph is very important. Reasons for starting a new paragraph include:

- To mark off the introduction and concluding paragraphs
- To signal a shift to a new idea or topic
- To indicate an important shift in time or place
- To explain a point in additional detail
- To highlight a comparison, contrast, or cause and effect relationship

A smooth flow of sentences and paragraphs without gaps, shifts, or bumps will lead to paragraph **coherence**. Ties between old and new information can be smoothed using several methods:

- **Linking ideas clearly**, from the topic sentence to the body of the paragraph, is essential for a smooth transition. The topic sentence states the main point, and this should be followed by specific details, examples, and illustrations that support the topic sentence. The support may be direct or indirect. In **indirect support**, the illustrations and examples may support a sentence that in turn supports the topic directly.
- The **repetition of key words** adds coherence to a paragraph. To avoid dull language, variations of the key words may be used.
- **Parallel structures** are often used within sentences to emphasize the similarity of ideas and connect sentences giving similar information.
- Maintaining a **consistent verb tense** throughout the paragraph helps. Shifting tenses affects the smooth flow of words and can disrupt the coherence of the paragraph.

After the introduction of a passage, a series of body paragraphs will carry a message through to the conclusion. Each paragraph should be **unified around a main point**. Normally, a good topic sentence summarizes the paragraph's main point. A topic sentence is a general sentence that gives an introduction to the paragraph.

The sentences that follow support the topic sentence. However, though it is usually the first sentence, the topic sentence can come as the final sentence to the paragraph if the earlier sentences give a clear explanation of the paragraph's topic. This allows the topic sentence to function as a concluding sentence. Overall, the paragraphs need to stay true to the main point. This means that any unnecessary sentences that do not advance the main point should be removed.

The main point of a paragraph requires adequate development (i.e., a substantial paragraph that covers the main point). A paragraph of two or three sentences does not cover a main point. This is especially true when the main point of the paragraph gives strong support to the argument of the thesis. An occasional short paragraph is fine as a transitional device. However, a well-developed argument will have paragraphs with more than a few sentences.

A **paragraph of narration** tells a story or a part of a story. Normally, the sentences are arranged in chronological order (i.e., the order that the events happened). However, flashbacks (i.e., an anecdote from an earlier time) can be included.

A **descriptive paragraph** makes a verbal portrait of a person, place, or thing. When specific details are used that appeal to one or more of the senses (i.e., sight, sound, smell, taste, and touch), authors give readers a sense of being present in the moment.

A **process paragraph** is related to time order (i.e., First, you open the bottle. Second, you pour the liquid, etc.). Usually, this describes a process or teaches readers how to perform a process.

Comparing two things draws attention to their similarities and indicates a number of differences. When authors contrast, they focus only on differences. Both comparing and contrasting may be done point-by-point, noting both the similarities and differences of each point, or in sequential paragraphs, where you discuss all the similarities and then all the differences, or vice versa.

Most readers find that their comfort level for a paragraph is between 100 and 200 words. Shorter paragraphs cause too much starting and stopping and give a choppy effect. Paragraphs that are too long often test the attention span of readers. Two notable exceptions to this rule exist. In scientific or scholarly papers, longer paragraphs suggest seriousness and depth. In journalistic writing, constraints are placed on paragraph size by the narrow columns in a newspaper format.

The first and last paragraphs of a text will usually be the introduction and conclusion. These special-purpose paragraphs are likely to be shorter than paragraphs in the body of the work. Paragraphs in the body of the essay follow the subject's outline (e.g., one paragraph per point in short essays and a group of paragraphs per point in longer works). Some ideas require more development than others, so it is good for a writer to remain flexible. A paragraph of excessive length may be divided, and shorter ones may be combined.

English Conventions
© Mometrix Media - flashcardsecrets.com/louisiana
English I

Discuss the role of body paragraphs in an essay.

English Conventions
© Mometrix Media - flashcardsecrets.com/louisiana
English I

List methods of adding substance to paragraphs.

Visit *mometrix.com/academy* for a related video.
Enter video code: 682127

English Conventions
© Mometrix Media - flashcardsecrets.com/louisiana
English I

What are common types of paragraphs?

English Conventions
© Mometrix Media - flashcardsecrets.com/louisiana
English I

What are some reasons for starting a new paragraph?

English Conventions
© Mometrix Media - flashcardsecrets.com/louisiana
English I

Describe the use of different lengths of paragraphs.

English Conventions
© Mometrix Media - flashcardsecrets.com/louisiana
English I

Discuss some strategies used for making paragraphs coherent.

A writer often begins the first paragraph of a paper by stating the **main idea** or point, also known as the **topic sentence**. The rest of the paragraph supplies particular details that develop and support the main point. One way to visualize the relationship between the main point and supporting information is by considering a table: the tabletop is the main point, and each of the table's legs is a supporting detail or group of details. Both professional authors and students can benefit from planning their writing by first making an outline of the topic. Outlines facilitate quick identification of the main point and supporting details without having to wade through the additional language that will exist in the fully developed essay, article, or paper. Outlining can also help readers to analyze a piece of existing writing for the same reason. The outline first summarizes the main idea in one sentence. Then, below that, it summarizes the supporting details in a numbered list. Writing the paper then consists of filling in the outline with detail, writing a paragraph for each supporting point, and adding an introduction and conclusion.

Technology makes managing written work more convenient. Digitally storing documents keeps everything in one place and is easy to reference. Digital storage also makes sharing work easier, as documents can be attached to an email or stored online. This also allows writers to publish their work easily, as they can electronically submit it to other publications or freely post it to a personal blog, profile, or website.

The thesis is the main idea of the essay. A temporary thesis, or working thesis, should be established early in the writing process because it will serve to keep the writer focused as ideas develop. This temporary thesis is subject to change as you continue to write.

The temporary thesis has two parts: a **topic** (i.e., the focus of your essay based on the prompt) and a **comment**. The comment makes an important point about the topic. A temporary thesis should be interesting and specific. Also, you need to limit the topic to a manageable scope. These three questions are useful tools to measure the effectiveness of any temporary thesis:

- Does the focus of my essay have enough interest to hold an audience?
- Is the focus of my essay specific enough to generate interest?
- Is the focus of my essay manageable for the time limit? Too broad? Too narrow?

The thesis should be a generalization rather than a fact because the thesis prepares readers for facts and details that support the thesis. The process of bringing the thesis into sharp focus may help in outlining major sections of the work. Once the thesis and introduction are complete, you can address the body of the work.

The purpose of the introduction is to capture the reader's attention and announce the essay's main idea. Normally, the introduction contains 50-80 words, or 3-5 sentences. An introduction can begin with an interesting quote, a question, or a strong opinion—something that will **engage** the reader's interest and prompt them to keep reading. If you are writing your essay to a specific prompt, your introduction should include a **restatement or summarization** of the prompt so that the reader will have some context for your essay. Finally, your introduction should briefly state your **thesis or main idea**: the primary thing you hope to communicate to the reader through your essay. Don't try to include all of the details and nuances of your thesis, or all of your reasons for it, in the introduction. That's what the rest of the essay is for!

In an essay's introduction, the writer establishes the thesis and may indicate how the rest of the piece will be structured. In the body of the piece, the writer **elaborates** upon, **illustrates**, and **explains** the **thesis statement**. How writers arrange supporting details and their choices of paragraph types are development techniques. Writers may give examples of the concept introduced in the thesis statement. If the subject includes a cause-and-effect relationship, the author may explain its causality. A writer will explain or analyze the main idea of the piece throughout the body, often by presenting arguments for the veracity or credibility of the thesis statement. Writers may use development to define or clarify ambiguous terms. Paragraphs within the body may be organized using natural sequences, like space and time. Writers may employ **inductive reasoning**, using multiple details to establish a generalization or causal relationship, or **deductive reasoning**, proving a generalized hypothesis or proposition through a specific example or case.

Throughout your essay, the thesis should be **explained clearly and supported** adequately by additional arguments. The thesis sentence needs to contain a clear statement of the purpose of your essay and a comment about the thesis. With the thesis statement, you have an opportunity to state what is noteworthy of this particular treatment of the prompt. Each sentence and paragraph should build on and support the thesis.

When you respond to the prompt, use parts of the passage to support your argument or defend your position. Using supporting evidence from the passage strengths your argument because readers can see your attention to the entire passage and your response to the details and facts within the passage. You can use facts, details, statistics, and direct quotations from the passage to uphold your position. Be sure to point out which information comes from the original passage and base your argument around that evidence.

English Conventions
© Mometrix Media - flashcardsecrets.com/louisiana
English I

Discuss how technology adds ease to the writing process and how it can be used to publish written work.

English Conventions
© Mometrix Media - flashcardsecrets.com/louisiana
English I

Describe the relationship between the topic sentence and supporting details in a paragraph. Discuss the benefits of making an outline and how the topic sentence and supporting details fit into an outline.

English Conventions
© Mometrix Media - flashcardsecrets.com/louisiana
English I

Discuss some things to consider when writing the introduction for an essay or other piece of writing. Give some sequential instructions for writing an introduction.

Visit *mometrix.com/academy* for a related video.
Enter video code: 961328

English Conventions
© Mometrix Media - flashcardsecrets.com/louisiana
English I

Discuss the thesis of an essay.

Visit *mometrix.com/academy* for a related video.
Enter video code: 691033

English Conventions
© Mometrix Media - flashcardsecrets.com/louisiana
English I

Discuss the importance of a clear and well-supported thesis and using supporting details throughout the composition.

English Conventions
© Mometrix Media - flashcardsecrets.com/louisiana
English I

Summarize some general examples of how to develop the body of a written essay or composition.

Visit *mometrix.com/academy* for a related video.
Enter video code: 724590

The **editing or proofreading stage** is focused specifically on improving the grammar and punctuation of the composition. The writer should read each paragraph closely and slowly to identify and fix any grammatical, spelling, or punctuation errors. Some of the worst offenders include subject-verb agreement in complex sentences, changes in tense throughout the document, and changes in perspective (first, second, or third person) or tone (professional, casual, opinionated, etc.). When writing at home, it is often helpful to have a friend or family member look for errors as well. Finally, this phase involves looking for very small errors, so multiple passes should be taken to catch as many problems as possible. One good rule of thumb is to keep reading through the whole document until a full read-through can be accomplished without finding any more errors.

However you approach writing, you may find comfort in knowing that the revision process can occur in any order. The **recursive writing process** is not as difficult as the phrase may make it seem. Simply put, the recursive writing process means that you may need to revisit steps after completing other steps. It also implies that the steps are not required to take place in any certain order. Indeed, you may find that planning, drafting, and revising can all take place at about the same time. The writing process involves moving back and forth between planning, drafting, and revising, followed by more planning, more drafting, and more revising until the writing is satisfactory.

Word processors also benefit the revising, editing, and proofreading stages of the writing process. Most of these programs indicate errors in spelling and grammar, allowing users to catch minor errors and correct them quickly. There are also websites designed to help writers by analyzing text for deeper errors, such as poor sentence structure, inappropriate complexity, lack of sentence variety, and style issues. These websites can help users fix errors they may not know to look for or may have simply missed. As writers finish these steps, they may benefit from checking their work for any plagiarism. There are several websites and programs that compare text to other documents and publications across the internet and detect any similarities within the text. These websites show the source of the similar information, so users know whether or not they referenced the source and unintentionally plagiarized its contents.

The **revision stage** is when the writer reads back through his or her work and looks for big-picture issues that affect **clarity** and **cohesion**. These can include organizational issues or flaws in logical flow. Writers should look back through their work to find any assertions or arguments that may be misplaced or lacking in support. They should look also through their work to find any information that does not contribute to the main idea or goal of the composition. Beginning writers may find it difficult to clearly communicate more than two or three main points in their arguments. If this is the case, these writers should eliminate information that detracts from those main points. In this stage, clarity is often more important than comprehensiveness.

The **publishing stage** refers to putting the document into its final format and delivering it to the audience. This involves formatting the document for presentation. In research writing, the final document may need to conform to a specific publishing standard, such as MLA or APA. In literal publishing, this would also take the form of presenting the document to the final audience, which may involve physical printing or digital publication. Note that once a composition has been published, it is often difficult to change or retract. Before reaching the publishing stage, the writer should have looped through the drafting, revision, and editing process a few times to ensure the writer says exactly what he or she wants before putting it before the final audience.

For the planning and drafting stages of the writing process, word processors are a helpful tool. These programs also feature formatting tools, allowing users to create their own planning tools or create digital outlines that can be easily converted into sentences, paragraphs, or an entire essay draft. Online databases and references also complement the planning process by providing convenient access to information and sources for research. Word processors also allow users to keep up with their work and update it more easily than if they wrote their work by hand. Online word processors often allow users to collaborate, making group assignments more convenient. These programs also allow users to include illustrations or other supplemental media in their compositions.

English Conventions
© Mometrix Media - flashcardsecrets.com/louisiana
English I

Describe the revising stage of the writing process.

English Conventions
© Mometrix Media - flashcardsecrets.com/louisiana
English I

Describe the editing and proofreading stage of the writing process

English Conventions
© Mometrix Media - flashcardsecrets.com/louisiana
English I

Describe the publishing stage of the writing process

English Conventions
© Mometrix Media - flashcardsecrets.com/louisiana
English I

Define the recursive writing process.

Visit *mometrix.com/academy* for a related video.
Enter video code: 951611

English Conventions
© Mometrix Media - flashcardsecrets.com/louisiana
English I

List technology that can be used in the planning and drafting phase of the writing process and how it benefits writers.

English Conventions
© Mometrix Media - flashcardsecrets.com/louisiana
English I

List and define technology that can aid writers during the revising, editing, and proofreading steps in the writing process.

Bank
(noun): an establishment where money is held for savings or lending
(verb): to collect or pile up

Content
(noun): the topics that will be addressed within a book
(adjective): pleased or satisfied
(verb): to make someone pleased or satisfied

Fine
(noun): an amount of money that acts a penalty for an offense
(adjective): very small or thin
(adverb): in an acceptable way
(verb): to make someone pay money as a punishment

Homographs are words that share the same spelling, but have different meanings and sometimes different pronunciations. To figure out which meaning is being used, you should be looking for context clues. The context clues give hints to the meaning of the word. For example, the word *spot* has many meanings. It can mean "a place" or "a stain or blot." In the sentence "After my lunch, I saw a spot on my shirt," the word *spot* means "a stain or blot." The context clues of "After my lunch" and "on my shirt" guide you to this decision. A homograph is another type of homonym.

Produce
(noun): fruits and vegetables
(verb): to make or create something

Refuse
(noun): garbage or debris that has been thrown away
(verb): to not allow

Subject
(noun): an area of study
(verb): to force or subdue

Tear
(noun): a fluid secreted by the eyes
(verb): to separate or pull apart

Incense
(noun): a material that is burned in religious settings and makes a pleasant aroma
(verb): to frustrate or anger

Lead
(noun): the first or highest position
(noun): a heavy metallic element
(verb): to direct a person or group of followers
(adjective): containing lead

Object
(noun): a lifeless item that can be held and observed
(verb): to disagree

The **drafting stage** of the writing process involves taking the plan for the composition and filling out all of the main ideas for the composition. Some writers prefer to start by writing the introduction and write their whole composition from start to finish, while others may prefer writing the main body paragraphs first and then coming back to the introduction and conclusion. In any case, the drafting process is a first attempt at writing the whole composition from start to finish. A writer may succeed in communicating what he or she wants in the first draft, but it often takes writing **several drafts** before the ideas and arguments take their final form. By the end of the drafting stage, the composition should be close to its final organization with its arguments clearly identified, but it will still need organizational, grammatical, and formatting improvements to be called complete.

The **prewriting stage** is the part of the process in which the writer focuses on **generating ideas** and developing a broad plan for what he or she wants to accomplish. **Brainstorming** is the process of thinking about a topic and writing down every thought that comes to mind. Brainstorming may also take the form of asking questions that need to be answered by the composition. **Free writing** has a similar goal of writing about a topic in a continuous flow for a short span of time (e.g., 2 to 3 minutes). The goal of these exercises is not to produce high-quality, polished thoughts, but to generate leads to follow when the more structured writing happens later in the process. In research writing, the prewriting stage may also include doing a literature review and **collecting information** to use as evidence in arguments later on. When collecting information, it is important to take clear notes of where an idea was originally found so it can be cited later on. Another key aspect of the prewriting process is **planning phase**. This entails deciding on the overall topic, purpose, tone, and general organization for the rest of the composition. The planning process may involve using aids like outlines, Venn diagrams, flowcharts, and other visual models to help collect and organize information. The planning process does not set the whole composition in stone, but it does help structure the ideas to be written in the drafting phase.

English Conventions
© Mometrix Media - flashcardsecrets.com/louisiana
English I

Define homographs, and explain how to figure which meaning is being used.

English Conventions
© Mometrix Media - flashcardsecrets.com/louisiana
English I

What are the meanings of the following homograph examples: bank, content, and fine?

English Conventions
© Mometrix Media - flashcardsecrets.com/louisiana
English I

What are the meanings of the following homograph examples: incense, lead, and object?

English Conventions
© Mometrix Media - flashcardsecrets.com/louisiana
English I

What are the meanings of the following homograph examples: produce, refuse, subject, and tear?

English Conventions
© Mometrix Media - flashcardsecrets.com/louisiana
English I

Describe the prewriting stage of the writing process.

English Conventions
© Mometrix Media - flashcardsecrets.com/louisiana
English I

Describe the drafting stage of the writing process.

Then is an adverb that indicates sequence or order:
Example: I'm going to run to the library and then come home.

Than is special-purpose word used only for comparisons:
Example: Susie likes chips more than candy.

Knew is the past tense of *know*.
Example: I knew the answer.

New is an adjective that means something is current, has not been used, or is modern.
Example: This is my new phone.

Your is a pronoun that shows ownership.
Example: This is your moment to shine.

You're is a contraction of *you are*.
Example: Yes, you're correct.

Its is a pronoun that shows ownership.
Example: The guitar is in its case.

It's is a contraction of *it is*.
Example: It's an honor and a privilege to meet you.

Note: The *h* in honor is silent, so *honor* starts with the vowel sound *o*, which must have the article *an*.

There are two main reasons that *affect* and *effect* are so often confused: 1) both words can be used as either a noun or a verb, and 2) unlike most homophones, their usage and meanings are closely related to each other. Here is a quick rundown of the four usage options:

Affect (n): feeling, emotion, or mood that is displayed
Example: The patient had a flat *affect*. (i.e., his face showed little or no emotion)
Affect (v): to alter, to change, to influence
Example: The sunshine *affects* the plant's growth.
Effect (n): a result, a consequence
Example: What *effect* will this weather have on our schedule?
Effect (v): to bring about, to cause to be
Example: These new rules will *effect* order in the office.

The noun form of *affect* is rarely used outside of technical medical descriptions, so if a noun form is needed on the test, you can safely select *effect*. The verb form of *effect* is not as rare as the noun form of *affect*, but it's still not all that likely to show up on your test. If you need a verb and you can't decide which to use based on the definitions, choosing *affect* is your best bet.

Saw is the past-tense form of *see*.
Example: I saw a turtle on my walk this morning.

Seen is the past participle of *see*.
Example: I have seen this movie before.

English Conventions
© Mometrix Media - flashcardsecrets.com/louisiana
English I

Compare knew and new as homophones.

English Conventions
© Mometrix Media - flashcardsecrets.com/louisiana
English I

Differentiate between the following frequently confused words: then and than.

English Conventions
© Mometrix Media - flashcardsecrets.com/louisiana
English I

Compare its and it's as homophones.

English Conventions
© Mometrix Media - flashcardsecrets.com/louisiana
English I

Compare your and you're as homophones.

English Conventions
© Mometrix Media - flashcardsecrets.com/louisiana
English I

Compare saw and seen as homophones.

English Conventions
© Mometrix Media - flashcardsecrets.com/louisiana
English I

Discuss the usage of all forms of affect and effect.

The ellipsis mark has **three** periods (…) to show when **words have been removed** from a quotation. If a **full sentence or more** is removed from a quoted passage, you need to use **four** periods to show the removed text and the end punctuation mark. The ellipsis mark should not be used at the beginning of a quotation. The ellipsis mark should also not be used at the end of a quotation unless some words have been deleted from the end of the final sentence.

Example:
"Then he picked up the groceries…paid for them…later he went home."

Dashes are used to show a **break** or a **change in thought** in a sentence or to act as parentheses in a sentence. When typing, use two hyphens to make a dash. Do not put a space before or after the dash. The following are the functions of dashes:

1. to set off **parenthetical statements** or an **appositive with internal punctuation**
   Example: The three trees—oak, pine, and magnolia—are coming on a truck tomorrow.

2. to show a **break or change in tone or thought**
   Example: The first question—how silly of me—does not have a correct answer.

The words *which*, *that*, and *who* can act as **relative pronouns** to help clarify or describe a noun.

Which is used for things only.
Example: Andrew's car, *which is old and rusty*, broke down last week.

That is used for people or things. *That* is usually informal when used to describe people.
Example: Is this the only book *that Louis L'Amour wrote?*
Example: Is Louis L'Amour the author *that wrote Western novels?*

Who is used for people or for animals that have an identity or personality.
Example: Mozart was the composer *who wrote those operas.*
Example: John's dog, *who is called Max*, is large and fierce.

There are two main reasons to use brackets:

1. When **placing parentheses inside of parentheses**
   Example: The hero of this story, Paul Revere (a silversmith and industrialist [see Ch. 4]), rode through towns of Massachusetts to warn of advancing British troops.

2. When adding **clarification or detail** to a quotation that is **not part of the quotation**
   Example:
   The father explained, "My children are planning to attend my alma mater [State University]."

There can be an adjective, adverb, or pronoun. Often, *there* is used to show a place or to start a sentence.
Examples: I went there yesterday. | There is something in his pocket.

Their is a pronoun that is used to show ownership.
Examples: He is their father. | This is their fourth apology this week.

They're is a contraction of *they are.*
Example: Did you know that they're in town?

Homophones are words that sound alike (or similar) but have different **spellings** and **definitions**. A homophone is a type of **homonym**, which is a pair or group of words that are pronounced or spelled the same, but do not mean the same thing.

To can be an adverb or a preposition for showing direction, purpose, and relationship. See your dictionary for the many other ways to use *to* in a sentence.
Examples: I went to the store. | I want to go with you.

Too is an adverb that means *also, as well, very,* or *in excess.*
Examples: I can walk a mile too. | You have eaten too much.

Two is a number.
Example: You have two minutes left.

English Conventions
© Mometrix Media - flashcardsecrets.com/louisiana
English I

Describe the use of dashes in sentences.

English Conventions
© Mometrix Media - flashcardsecrets.com/louisiana
English I

Describe the use of an ellipsis.

English Conventions
© Mometrix Media - flashcardsecrets.com/louisiana
English I

Discuss the two main reasons to use brackets.

Visit *mometrix.com/academy* for a related video.
Enter video code: 727546

English Conventions
© Mometrix Media - flashcardsecrets.com/louisiana
English I

Differentiate between the following frequently confused words:
which, that, and who

English Conventions
© Mometrix Media - flashcardsecrets.com/louisiana
English I

Define homophones and compare to, too, and two as homophones.

English Conventions
© Mometrix Media - flashcardsecrets.com/louisiana
English I

Compare there, their, and they're as homophones.

Use quotation marks to close off **direct quotations** of a person's spoken or written words. Do not use quotation marks around indirect quotations. An indirect quotation gives someone's message without using the person's exact words. Use **single quotation marks** to close off a quotation inside a quotation.

  Direct Quote: Nancy said, "I am waiting for Henry to arrive."
  Indirect Quote: Henry said that he is going to be late to the meeting.
  Quote inside a Quote: The teacher asked, "Has everyone read 'The Gift of the Magi'?"

Quotation marks should be used around the titles of **short works**: newspaper and magazine articles, poems, short stories, songs, television episodes, radio programs, and subdivisions of books or websites.
Examples:
  "Rip Van Winkle" (short story by Washington Irving)
  "O Captain! My Captain!" (poem by Walt Whitman)

Parentheses are used for additional information. Also, they can be used to put labels for letters or numbers in a series. Parentheses should be not be used very often. If they are overused, parentheses can be a distraction instead of a help.

Examples:
  Extra Information: The rattlesnake (see Image 2) is a dangerous snake of North and South America.
  Series: Include in the email (1) your name, (2) your address, and (3) your question for the author.

Periods and commas are put **inside** quotation marks. Colons and semicolons are put **outside** the quotation marks. Question marks and exclamation points are placed inside quotation marks when they are part of a quote. When the question or exclamation mark goes with the whole sentence, the mark is left outside of the quotation marks.

Examples:
  Period and comma: We read "The Gift of the Magi," "The Skylight Room," and "The Cactus."
  Semicolon: They watched "The Nutcracker"; then, they went home.
  Exclamation mark that is a part of a quote: The crowd cheered, "Victory!"
  Question mark that goes with the whole sentence: Is your favorite short story "The Tell-Tale Heart"?

Although it is not standard usage, quotation marks are sometimes used to highlight **irony** or the use of words to mean something other than their dictionary definition. This type of usage should be employed sparingly, if at all.

Examples:
  The boss warned Frank that he was walking on "thin ice."
  (Frank is not walking on real ice. Instead, Frank is being warned to avoid mistakes.)
  The teacher thanked the young man for his "honesty."
  (In this example, the quotation marks around *honesty* show that the teacher does not believe the young man's explanation.)

Hyphens are used to **separate compound words**. Use hyphens in the following cases:
1. **Compound numbers** from 21 to 99 when written out in words
  Example: This team needs *twenty-five* points to win the game.

2. **Written-out fractions** that are used as **adjectives**
  Incorrect: *One-fourth* of the road is under construction.
  Correct: The recipe says that we need a *three-fourths* cup of butter.

3. Compound **adjectives that come before a noun**
  Incorrect: The dog was *well-fed* for his nap.
  Correct: The *well-fed* dog took a nap.

4. Unusual compound words that would be **hard to read** or **easily confused with other words**
  Examples: Semi-irresponsible | Anti-itch | Re-sort

Note: This is not a complete set of the rules for hyphens. A dictionary is the best tool for knowing if a compound word needs a hyphen.

An apostrophe is used to show **possession** or the **deletion of letters in contractions**. An apostrophe is not needed with the possessive pronouns *his, hers, its, ours, theirs, whose*, and *yours*.

  Singular Nouns: David's car | a book's theme | my brother's board game
  Plural Nouns that end with -*s*: the scissors' handle | boys' basketball
  Plural Nouns that end without -*s*: Men's department | the people's adventure

English Conventions
© Mometrix Media - flashcardsecrets.com/louisiana
English I

Discuss the use of parentheses.

Visit *mometrix.com/academy* for a related video.
Enter video code: 947743

English Conventions
© Mometrix Media - flashcardsecrets.com/louisiana
English I

Describe the use of quotation marks in quotations and in titles.

English Conventions
© Mometrix Media - flashcardsecrets.com/louisiana
English I

Discuss the use of quotation marks to indicate words being used ironically.

Visit *mometrix.com/academy* for a related video.
Enter video code: 884918

English Conventions
© Mometrix Media - flashcardsecrets.com/louisiana
English I

Discuss the placement of quotation marks in relation to periods, commas, semicolons, exclamation points, and question marks.

English Conventions
© Mometrix Media - flashcardsecrets.com/louisiana
English I

Describe the use of apostrophes.

Visit *mometrix.com/academy* for related videos.
Enter video codes: 213068 and 221438

English Conventions
© Mometrix Media - flashcardsecrets.com/louisiana
English I

Describe the use of hyphens with compound words.

Visit *mometrix.com/academy* for a related video.
Enter video code: 981632

The comma is a punctuation mark that can help you understand connections in a sentence. Not every sentence needs a comma. However, if a sentence needs a comma, you need to put it in the right place. A comma in the wrong place (or an absent comma) will make a sentence's meaning unclear.

These are some of the rules for commas:
- Use a comma **before a coordinating conjunction** joining independent clauses.
  Example: Bob caught three fish, and I caught two fish.
- Use a comma after an introductory phrase or an adverbial clause.
  Examples:
  After the final out, we went to a restaurant to celebrate.
  Studying the stars, I was surprised at the beauty of the sky.
- Use a comma between items in a series.
  Example: I will bring the turkey, the pie, and the coffee.
- Use a comma **between coordinate adjectives** not joined with *and*.
  Incorrect: The kind, brown dog followed me home.
  Correct: *The kind, loyal dog followed me home.*
  Not all adjectives are **coordinate** (i.e., equal or parallel). There are two simple ways to know if your adjectives are coordinate. One, you can join the adjectives with and: *The kind and loyal dog*. Two, you can change the order of the adjectives: *The loyal, kind dog.*

- Use commas when writing dates, addresses, geographical names, and titles.
  Examples:
  Date: *July 4, 1776*, is an important date to remember.
  Address: He is meeting me at *456 Delaware Avenue, Washington, D.C.*, tomorrow morning.
  Geographical Name *Paris, France*, is my favorite city.
  Title: John Smith, *PhD*, will be visiting your class today.
- Use commas to **separate expressions like *he said* and *she said*** if they appear between two parts of a quote.
  Examples:
  "I want you to know," he began, "that I always wanted the best for you."
  "You can start," Jane said, "with an apology."

The colon is used to call attention to the words that follow it. A colon must come after a **complete independent clause**. The rules for colons are as follows:
1. Use a colon after an independent clause to **make a list.**
   Example: I want to learn many languages: Spanish, German, and Italian.
2. Use a colon for **explanations** or to **give a quote.**
   Examples:
   Quote: He started with an idea: "We are able to do more than we imagine."
   Explanation: There is one thing that stands out on your resume: responsibility.
3. Use a colon **after the greeting in a formal letter**, to **show hours and minutes,** and to **separate a title and subtitle.**
   Examples:
   Greeting in a formal letter: Dear Sir: | To Whom It May Concern:
   Time: It is 3:14 p.m.
   Title: The essay is titled "America: A Short Introduction to a Modern Country."

Question marks should be used following a **direct question**. A polite request can be followed by a period instead of a question mark.
> **Direct Question**: What is for lunch today? | How are you? | Why is that the answer?
> **Polite Requests**: Can you please send me the item tomorrow. | Will you please walk with me on the track.

Exclamation marks are used after a word group or sentence that shows much feeling or has special importance. Exclamation marks should not be overused. They are saved for proper **exclamatory interjections**.
> Example: We're going to the finals! | You have a beautiful car! | "That's crazy!" she yelled.

- Use commas for **interjections** and **after *yes* and *no*** responses.
  Examples:
  Interjection: Oh, I had no idea. | Wow, you know how to play this game.
  Yes and No: *Yes*, I heard you. | *No*, I cannot come tomorrow.
- Use commas to separate nonessential modifiers and nonessential appositives.
  Examples:
  Nonessential Modifier: John Frank, who is coaching the team, was promoted today.
  Nonessential Appositive: Thomas Edison, an American inventor, was born in Ohio.
- Use commas to separate nouns of direct address, interrogative tags, and contrast.
  Examples:
  Direct Address: You, *John*, are my only hope in this moment.
  Interrogative Tag: This is the last time, *correct*?
  Contrast: You are my friend, *not my enemy*.

The semicolon is used to connect major sentence pieces of equal value. Some rules for semicolons include:
1. Use a semicolon **between closely connected independent clauses** that are not connected with a coordinating conjunction.
   Examples:
   She is outside; we are inside.
   You are right; we should go with your plan.
2. Use a semicolon **between independent clauses linked with a transitional word.**
   Examples:
   I think that we can agree on this; *however,* I am not sure about my friends.
   You are looking in the wrong places; *therefore,* you will not find what you need.
3. Use a semicolon **between items in a series that has internal punctuation.**
   Example: I have visited New York, New York; Augusta, Maine; and Baltimore, Maryland.

English Conventions
© Mometrix Media - flashcardsecrets.com/louisiana
English I

Discuss the use of question marks and exclamation marks.

Visit *mometrix.com/academy* for related videos.
Enter video codes: 118471 and 199367

English Conventions
© Mometrix Media - flashcardsecrets.com/louisiana
English I

Describe the use of commas in general and in the following situations:
before a coordinating conjunction
after an introductory phrase
between items in a series
between coordinate adjectives not joined with *and*

English Conventions
© Mometrix Media - flashcardsecrets.com/louisiana
English I

Describe the use of commas in the following situations:
after interjections and yes/no
separating nonessential modifiers
separating nouns of direct address

English Conventions
© Mometrix Media - flashcardsecrets.com/louisiana
English I

Describe the use of commas in the following situations:
dates, address, geographical names, and titles
he/she said in the middle of a quotation

Visit *mometrix.com/academy* for a related video.
Enter video code: 786797

English Conventions
© Mometrix Media - flashcardsecrets.com/louisiana
English I

Describe the use of semicolons.

Visit *mometrix.com/academy* for a related video.
Enter video code: 370605

English Conventions
© Mometrix Media - flashcardsecrets.com/louisiana
English I

Discuss the use of colons.

Visit *mometrix.com/academy* for a related video.
Enter video code: 868673

A dangling modifier is a dependent clause or verbal phrase that does not have a **clear logical connection** to a word in the sentence.
Example:

Incorrect: Reading each magazine article, the stories caught my attention.
The word *stories* cannot be modified by *Reading each magazine article*. People can read, but stories cannot read. Therefore, the subject of the sentence must be a person.

Corrected: Reading each magazine article, I was entertained by the stories.
Example:

Incorrect: Ever since childhood, my grandparents
have visited me for Christmas.
The speaker in this sentence can't have been visited by her grandparents when *they* were children, since she wouldn't have been born yet. Either the modifier should be clarified or the sentence should be rearranged to specify whose childhood is being referenced.

Clarified: Ever since I was a child, my grandparents have visited for Christmas.
Rearranged: I have enjoyed my grandparents
visiting for Christmas, ever since childhood.

A split infinitive occurs when a modifying word comes between the word *to* and the verb that pairs with *to*.

Example: To *clearly* explain vs. *To explain* clearly | To *softly* sing vs. *To sing* softly

Though considered improper by some, split infinitives may provide better clarity and simplicity in some cases than the alternatives. As such, avoiding them should not be considered a universal rule.

Use a period to end all sentences except direct questions and exclamations. Periods are also used for abbreviations.

Examples: 3 p.m. | 2 a.m. | Mr. Jones | Mrs. Stevens | Dr. Smith | Bill, Jr. | Pennsylvania Ave.

Note: An abbreviation is a shortened form of a word or phrase.

Make one clause dependent: This is the easiest way to make the sentence correct and more interesting at the same time. It's often as simple as adding a subordinating word between the two clauses or before the first clause.

Example:
    Incorrect: I finally made it to the store and I bought some eggs.
    Corrected: When I finally made it to the store, I bought some eggs.

Reduce to one clause with a compound verb: If both clauses have the same subject, remove the subject from the second clause, and you now have just one clause with a compound verb.

Example:
    Incorrect: The drive to New York takes ten hours, it makes me very tired.
    Corrected: The drive to New York takes ten hours and makes me very tired.

Note: While these are the simplest ways to correct a run-on sentence, often the best way is to completely reorganize the thoughts in the sentence and rewrite it.

Because modifiers are grammatically versatile, they can be put in many different places within the structure of a sentence. The danger of this versatility is that a modifier can accidentally be placed where it is modifying the wrong word or where it is not clear which word it is modifying.

Example:
Incorrect: She read the book to a crowd
that was filled with beautiful pictures.
The book was filled with beautiful pictures, not the crowd.
Corrected: She read the book
that was filled with beautiful pictures to a crowd.
Example:

Ambiguous: Derek saw a bus nearly hit a man on his way to work.
Was Derek on his way to work or was the other man?
Derek: On his way to work, Derek saw a bus nearly hit a man.
The other man: Derek saw a bus nearly hit a
man who was on his way to work.

Standard English allows **two negatives** only when a **positive** meaning is intended. For example, *The team was not displeased with their performance*. Double negatives to emphasize negation are not used in standard English.

Negative modifiers (e.g., never, no, and not) should not be paired with other negative modifiers or negative words (e.g., none, nobody, nothing, or neither). The modifiers *hardly, barely*, and *scarcely* are also considered negatives in standard English, so they should not be used with other negatives.

English Conventions
© Mometrix Media - flashcardsecrets.com/louisiana
English I

Explain how to correct run-on sentences without combining or separating clauses.

Visit *mometrix.com/academy* for a related video.
Enter video code: 541989

English Conventions
© Mometrix Media - flashcardsecrets.com/louisiana
English I

Describe dangling modifiers and how to correct them.

English Conventions
© Mometrix Media - flashcardsecrets.com/louisiana
English I

Discuss modifiers and their uses.

English Conventions
© Mometrix Media - flashcardsecrets.com/louisiana
English I

Define and discuss split infinitives.

English Conventions
© Mometrix Media - flashcardsecrets.com/louisiana
English I

Discuss the use of double negatives.

English Conventions
© Mometrix Media - flashcardsecrets.com/louisiana
English I

Discuss the use of periods for end punctuation and for abbreviations.

Sentences are classified by structure based on the type and number of clauses present. The four classifications of sentence structure are the following:

Simple: A simple sentence has one independent clause with no dependent clauses. A simple sentence may have **compound elements** (i.e., compound subject or verb).

Examples:

single subject | single verb
Judy watered the lawn.

compound subject | single verb
Judy and Alan watered the lawn.

single subject | compound verb | compound verb
Judy watered the lawn and pulled weeds.

compound subject | compound verb | compound verb
Judy and Alan watered the lawn and pulled weeds.

There are four types of sentences: declarative, imperative, interrogative, and exclamatory.

A **declarative** sentence states a fact and ends with a period.
    The football game starts at seven o'clock.

An **imperative** sentence tells someone to do something and generally ends with a period. An urgent command might end with an exclamation point instead.
    Don't forget to buy your ticket.

An **interrogative** sentence asks a question and ends with a question mark.
    Are you going to the game on Friday?

An **exclamatory** sentence shows strong emotion and ends with an exclamation point.
    I can't believe we won the game!

Sentence variety is important to consider when writing an essay or speech. A variety of sentence lengths and types creates rhythm, makes a passage more engaging, and gives writers an opportunity to demonstrate their writing style. Writing that uses the same length or type of sentence without variation can be boring or difficult to read. To evaluate a passage for effective sentence variety, it is helpful to note whether the passage contains diverse sentence structures and lengths. It is also important to pay attention to the way each sentence starts and avoid beginning with the same words or phrases.

Compound: A compound sentence has two or more independent clauses with no dependent clauses. Usually, the independent clauses are joined with a comma and a coordinating conjunction or with a semicolon.
Examples:

independent clause | independent clause
The time has come, and we are ready.

independent clause | independent clause
I woke up at dawn; the sun was just coming up.

Complex: A complex sentence has one independent clause and at least one dependent clause.
Examples:

dependent clause | independent clause
Although he had the flu, Harry went to work.

independent clause | dependent clause
Marcia got married, after she finished college.

Compound-Complex: A compound-complex sentence has at least two independent clauses and at least one dependent clause.
Examples:

independent clause | dependent clause | independent clause
John is my friend who went to India, and he brought back souvenirs.

independent clause | independent clause | dependent clause
You may not realize this, but we heard the music that you played last night.

Run-on sentences consist of multiple independent clauses that have not been joined together properly. Run-on sentences can be corrected in several different ways:

Join clauses properly: This can be done with a comma and coordinating conjunction, with a semicolon, or with a colon or dash if the second clause is explaining something in the first.

Example:
    Incorrect: I went on the trip, we visited lots of castles.
    Corrected: I went on the trip, and we visited lots of castles.

Split into separate sentences: This correction is most effective when the independent clauses are very long or when they are not closely related.

Example:
    Incorrect: The drive to New York takes ten hours, my uncle lives in Boston.
    Corrected: The drive to New York takes ten hours. My uncle lives in Boston.

Recall that a group of words must contain at least one **independent clause** in order to be considered a sentence. If it doesn't contain even one independent clause, it would be called a **sentence fragment**.

The appropriate process for **repairing** a sentence fragment depends on what type of fragment it is. If the fragment is a dependent clause, it can sometimes be as simple as removing a subordinating word (e.g., when, because, if) from the beginning of the fragment. Alternatively, a dependent clause can be incorporated into a closely related neighboring sentence. If the fragment is missing some required part, like a subject or a verb, the fix might be as simple as adding the missing part.

Examples:
    Fragment: Because he wanted to sail the Mediterranean.
    Removed subordinating word: He wanted to sail the Mediterranean.
    Combined with another sentence: Because he wanted to sail the Mediterranean, he booked a Greek island cruise.

English Conventions
© Mometrix Media - flashcardsecrets.com/louisiana
English I

Discuss types of sentences.

English Conventions
© Mometrix Media - flashcardsecrets.com/louisiana
English I

Describe simple sentence structure.

English Conventions
© Mometrix Media - flashcardsecrets.com/louisiana
English I

Describe compound sentence structure, complex sentence structure, and compound-complex sentence structure.

Visit *mometrix.com/academy* for a related video.
Enter video code: 700478

English Conventions
© Mometrix Media - flashcardsecrets.com/louisiana
English I

Discuss sentence variety and how to evaluate a passage for effective sentence variety.

English Conventions
© Mometrix Media - flashcardsecrets.com/louisiana
English I

Discuss sentence fragments.

English Conventions
© Mometrix Media - flashcardsecrets.com/louisiana
English I

Explain run-on sentences and how to correct them by combining or separating clauses.

A **gerund** is a type of verbal that always functions as a **noun**. Like present participles, gerunds always end with *-ing*, but they can be easily distinguished from one another by the part of speech they represent (participles always function as adjectives). Since a gerund or gerund phrase always functions as a noun, it can be used as the subject of a sentence, the predicate nominative, or the object of a verb or preposition.

Examples:

gerund

We want to be known for teaching the poor.

object of preposition

gerund

Coaching this team is the best job of my life.

subject

gerund

We like practicing our songs in the basement.

object of verb

A **participle** is a type of verbal that always functions as an adjective. The present participle always ends with *-ing*. Past participles end with *-d, -ed, -n,* or *-t*.

verb | present participle | past participle

Examples: dance | dancing | danced

Participial phrases most often come right before or right after the noun or pronoun that they modify.
Examples:

participial phrase

Shipwrecked on an island, the boys started to fish for food.

participial phrase

Having been seated for five hours, we got out of the car to stretch our legs.

participial phrase

Praised for their work, the group accepted the first-place trophy.

An **appositive** is a word or phrase that is used to explain or rename nouns or pronouns. Noun phrases, gerund phrases, and infinitive phrases can all be used as appositives.
Examples:

appositive

Terriers, hunters at heart, have been dressed up to look like lap dogs.
The noun phrase *hunters at heart* renames the noun *terriers*.

appositive

His plan, to save and invest his money, was proven as a safe approach.
The infinitive phrase explains what the plan is.

Appositive phrases can be **essential** or **nonessential**. An appositive phrase is essential if the person, place, or thing being described or renamed is too general for its meaning to be understood without the appositive.

Examples:
Two of America's Founding Fathers,

essential

George Washington and Thomas Jefferson, served as presidents.

George Washington and Thomas Jefferson,

nonessential

two Founding Fathers, served as presidents.

An **infinitive** is a type of verbal that can function as a noun, an adjective, or an adverb. An infinitive is made of the word *to* and the basic form of the verb. As with all other types of verbal phrases, an infinitive phrase includes the verbal itself and all of its complements or modifiers.

Examples:

infinitive

To join the team is my goal in life.

noun

infinitive

The animals have enough food to eat for the night.

adjective

infinitive

People lift weights to exercise their muscles.

adverb

When multiple items or ideas are presented in a sentence in series, such as in a list, the items or ideas must be stated in grammatically equivalent ways. In other words, if one idea is stated in gerund form, the second cannot be stated in infinitive form. For example, to write, *I enjoy reading and to study* would be incorrect. An infinitive and a gerund are not equivalent. Instead, you should write *I enjoy reading and studying*. In lists of more than two, all items must be parallel.
Example:
    Incorrect: He stopped at the office, grocery store, and the pharmacy before heading home.
    The first and third items in the list of places include the article *the*, so the second item needs it as well.
    Correct: He stopped at the office, *the* grocery store, and the pharmacy before heading home.
Example:
    Incorrect: While vacationing in Europe, she went biking, skiing, and climbed mountains.
    The first and second items in the list are gerunds, so the third item must be as well.
    Correct: While vacationing in Europe, she went biking, skiing, and *mountain climbing*.

An absolute phrase is a phrase that consists of **a noun followed by a participle**. An absolute phrase provides **context** to what is being described in the sentence, but it does not modify or explain any particular word; it is essentially independent.

Examples:

noun | participle

The alarm ringing, he pushed the snooze button.

absolute phrase

noun | participle

The music paused, she continued to dance through the crowd.

absolute phrase

English Conventions
© Mometrix Media - flashcardsecrets.com/louisiana
English I

Describe the use of participles and participial phrases.

English Conventions
© Mometrix Media - flashcardsecrets.com/louisiana
English I

Describe the use of gerunds and gerund phrases.

English Conventions
© Mometrix Media - flashcardsecrets.com/louisiana
English I

Describe the use of infinitives and infinitive phrases.

Visit *mometrix.com/academy* for a related video.
Enter video code: 915480

English Conventions
© Mometrix Media - flashcardsecrets.com/louisiana
English I

Define and discuss the use of appositives.

English Conventions
© Mometrix Media - flashcardsecrets.com/louisiana
English I

Define and discuss the use of absolute phrases.

English Conventions
© Mometrix Media - flashcardsecrets.com/louisiana
English I

Explain the use of proper parallel structures in sentences.

Visit *mometrix.com/academy* for a related video.
Enter video code: 831988

An **adverb clause** is a dependent clause that modifies a verb, adjective, or adverb. In sentences with multiple dependent clauses, adverb clauses are usually placed immediately before or after the independent clause. An adverb clause is introduced with words such as *after, although, as, before, because, if, since, so, unless, when, where,* and *while.*

Examples:

adverb
clause
When you walked outside, I called the manager.

adverb
clause
I will go with you unless you want to stay.

When two related ideas are not of equal importance, the ideal way to combine them is to make the more important idea an independent clause and the less important idea a dependent or subordinate clause. This is called **subordination**.

Example:
Separate ideas: The team had a perfect regular season. The team lost the championship.
Subordinated: Despite having a perfect regular season, *the team lost the championship.*

An **adjective clause** is a dependent clause that modifies a noun or a pronoun. Adjective clauses begin with a relative pronoun (*who, whose, whom, which,* and *that*) or a relative adverb (*where, when,* and *why*).
Also, adjective clauses come after the noun that the clause needs to explain or rename. This is done to have a clear connection to the independent clause.

Examples:

independent   adjective
clause   clause
I learned the reason why I won the award.

independent   adjective
clause   clause
This is the place where I started my first job.

An adjective clause can be an essential or nonessential clause. An essential clause is very important to the sentence. **Essential clauses** explain or define a person or thing. **Nonessential clauses** give more information about a person or thing but are not necessary to define them. Nonessential clauses are set off with commas while essential clauses are not.

Examples:

essential
clause
A person who works hard at first can often rest later in life.

nonessential
clause
Neil Armstrong, who walked on the moon, is my hero.

A **noun clause** is a dependent clause that can be used as a subject, object, or complement. Noun clauses begin with words such as *how, that, what, whether, which, who,* and *why.* These words can also come with an adjective clause. Unless the noun clause is being used as the subject of the sentence, it should come after the verb of the independent clause.

Examples:

noun
clause
The real mystery is how you avoided serious injury.

noun
clause
What you learn from each other depends on your honesty with others.

A **verbal** is a word or phrase that is formed from a verb but does not function as a verb. Depending on its particular form, it may be used as a noun, adjective, or adverb. A verbal does **not** replace a verb in a sentence.

Examples:

verb
Correct: Walk a mile daily.
This is a complete sentence with the implied subject *you.*

verbal
Incorrect: To walk a mile.
This is not a sentence since there is no functional verb.

There are three types of verbal: **participles, gerunds,** and **infinitives**. Each type of verbal has a corresponding **phrase** that consists of the verbal itself along with any complements or modifiers.

A phrase is a group of words that functions as a single part of speech, usually a noun, adjective, or adverb. A **phrase** is not a complete thought, but it adds detail or explanation to a sentence, or renames something within the sentence.

Prepositional Phrases
One of the most common types of phrases is the prepositional phrase. A **prepositional phrase** begins with a preposition and ends with a noun or pronoun that is the object of the preposition. Normally, the prepositional phrase functions as an **adjective** or an **adverb** within the sentence.

Examples:

prepositional
phrase
The picnic is on the blanket.

prepositional
phrase
I am sick with a fever today.

prepositional
phrase
Among the many flowers, John found a four-leaf clover.

English Conventions
© Mometrix Media - flashcardsecrets.com/louisiana
English I

Define and discuss the use of adjective clauses.

Visit *mometrix.com/academy* for a related video.
Enter video code: 520888

English Conventions
© Mometrix Media - flashcardsecrets.com/louisiana
English I

Define and discuss the use of adverb clauses.

English Conventions
© Mometrix Media - flashcardsecrets.com/louisiana
English I

Define and discuss the use of noun clauses.

English Conventions
© Mometrix Media - flashcardsecrets.com/louisiana
English I

Describe the use of subordinate clauses to show relative importance.

English Conventions
© Mometrix Media - flashcardsecrets.com/louisiana
English I

Define and discuss the use of phrases, including prepositional phrases.

English Conventions
© Mometrix Media - flashcardsecrets.com/louisiana
English I

Define and discuss the use of verbals including verbal phrases.

To determine which is the correct pronoun to use in a compound subject or object, try each pronoun **alone** in place of the compound in the sentence. Your knowledge of pronouns will tell you which one is correct.

Example:
> Bob and (I, me) will be going.
> Test: (1) *I will be going* or (2) *Me will be going*. The second choice cannot be correct because *me* cannot be used as the subject of a sentence. Instead, *me* is used as an object.
> **Answer**: Bob and I will be going.

When a pronoun is used with a noun immediately following (as in "we boys"), try the sentence **without the added noun**.
Example:
> (We/Us) boys played football last year.
> Test: (1) *We played football last year* or (2) *Us played football last year*. Again, the second choice cannot be correct because *us* cannot be used as a subject of a sentence. Instead, *us* is used as an object.
> **Answer**: We boys played football last year.

Some pronouns change their form by their placement in a sentence. A pronoun that is a **subject** in a sentence comes in the **subjective case**. Pronouns that serve as **objects** appear in the **objective case**. Finally, the pronouns that are used as **possessives** appear in the **possessive case**.

Examples:
> **Subjective case**: *He* is coming to the show.
> (The pronoun *He* is the subject of the sentence.)
> **Objective case**: Josh drove *him* to the airport.
> (The pronoun *him* is the object of the sentence.)
> **Possessive case**: The flowers are *mine*.
> (The pronoun *mine* shows ownership of the flowers.)

A clause is a group of words that contains both a subject and a predicate (verb). There are two types of clauses: independent and dependent. An **independent clause** contains a complete thought, while a **dependent (or subordinate) clause** does not. A dependent clause includes a subject and a verb, and may also contain objects or complements, but it cannot stand as a complete thought without being joined to an independent clause. Dependent clauses function within sentences as adjectives, adverbs, or nouns.

Example:
> independent clause | dependent clause
> I am running because I want to stay in shape.

The clause *I am running* is an independent clause: it has a subject and a verb, and it gives a complete thought. The clause *because I want to stay in shape* is a dependent clause: it has a subject and a verb, but it does not express a complete thought. It adds detail to the independent clause to which it is attached.

The **antecedent** is the noun that has been replaced by a pronoun. A pronoun and its antecedent **agree** when they have the same number (singular or plural) and gender (male, female, or neutral).

Examples:

> **Singular agreement**: John (antecedent) came into town, and he (pronoun) played for us.

> **Plural agreement**: John and Rick (antecedent) came into town, and they (pronoun) played for us.

A pronoun should point clearly to the **antecedent**. Here is how a pronoun reference can be unhelpful if it is puzzling or not directly stated.

> **Unhelpful**: Ron and Jim (antecedent) went to the store, and he (pronoun) bought soda.

> Who bought soda? Ron or Jim?

> **Helpful**: Jim (antecedent) went to the store, and he (pronoun) bought soda.

> The sentence is clear. Jim bought the soda.

The word *who* is a subjective-case pronoun that can be used as a **subject**. The word *whom* is an objective-case pronoun that can be used as an **object**. The words *who* and *whom* are common in subordinate clauses or in questions.

Examples:

> He knows who (subject) wants (verb) to come.

> He knows the man whom (object) we want (verb) at the party.

English Conventions
© Mometrix Media - flashcardsecrets.com/louisiana
English I

Discuss pronoun-antecedents agreement.

English Conventions
© Mometrix Media - flashcardsecrets.com/louisiana
English I

Explain proper pronoun use in a compound subject or object.

Visit *mometrix.com/academy* for a related video.
Enter video code: 666500

English Conventions
© Mometrix Media - flashcardsecrets.com/louisiana
English I

Give an example to illustrate clear pronoun reference.

English Conventions
© Mometrix Media - flashcardsecrets.com/louisiana
English I

Explain how pronouns change form.

English Conventions
© Mometrix Media - flashcardsecrets.com/louisiana
English I

Explain the use of the words who and whom.

English Conventions
© Mometrix Media - flashcardsecrets.com/louisiana
English I

Discuss the two types of clauses.

Visit *mometrix.com/academy* for a related video.
Enter video code: 556903

An indefinite pronoun is a pronoun that does not refer to a specific noun. Different indefinite pronouns may only function as a singular noun, only function as a plural noun, or change depending on how they are used.

Always Singular
Pronouns such as *each, either, everybody, anybody, somebody,* and *nobody* are always singular.

Examples:

[singular subject] Each of the runners [singular verb] has a different bib number.

[singular verb] Is [singular subject] either of you ready for the game?

Note: The words *each* and *either* can also be used as adjectives (e.g., *each* person is unique). When one of these adjectives modifies the subject of a sentence, it is always a singular subject.

[singular subject] Everybody [singular verb] grows a day older every day.

[singular subject] Anybody [singular verb] is welcome to bring a tent.

Some nouns are **singular in meaning but plural in form**: news, mathematics, physics, and economics.
    The *news is* coming on now.
    Mathematics is my favorite class.

Some nouns are plural in form and meaning, and have **no singular equivalent**: scissors and pants.
    Do these *pants come* with a shirt?
    The *scissors are* for my project.

Mathematical operations are **irregular** in their construction, but are normally considered to be **singular in meaning**.
    One plus one is two.
    Three times three is nine.

Note: Look to your **dictionary** for help when you aren't sure whether a noun with a plural form has a singular or plural meaning.

Verbs may be classified as either action verbs or linking verbs. A linking verb is so named because it links the subject to words in the predicate that describe or define the subject. These words are called predicate nominatives (if nouns or pronouns) or predicate adjectives (if adjectives).

Examples:

[subject] My father is a [predicate nominative] lawyer.

[subject] Your mother is [predicate adjective] patient.

A compound subject is formed when two or more nouns joined by *and, or,* or *nor* jointly act as the subject of the sentence.

Joined by And
When a compound subject is joined by *and,* it is treated as a plural subject and requires a plural verb.
Examples:

[plural subject] You and Jon [plural verb] are invited to come to my house.

The [plural subject] pencil and paper [plural verb] belong to me.

Joined by Or/Nor
For a compound subject joined by *or* or *nor,* the verb must agree in number with the part of the subject that is closest to the verb (italicized in the examples below).
Examples:

[subject] Today or tomorrow [verb] is the day.

[subject] Stan or Phil [verb] wants to read the book.

[subject] Neither the pen nor the book [verb] is on the desk.

[subject] Either the blanket or pillows [verb] arrive this afternoon.

Always Plural
Pronouns such as *both, several,* and *many* are always plural.

Examples:

[plural subject] Both of the siblings [plural verb] were too tired to argue.

[plural subject] Many [plural verb] have tried, but none have succeeded.

Depend on Context
Pronouns such as some, any, all, none, more, and most can be either singular or plural depending on what they are representing in the context of the sentence.

Examples:

[singular subject] All of my dog's food [singular verb] was still there in his bowl.

By the end of the night, [plural subject] all of my guests [plural verb] were already excited about coming to my next party.

A complement is a noun, pronoun, or adjective that is used to give more information about the subject or verb in the sentence.

Direct Objects
A direct object is a noun or pronoun that takes or receives the **action** of a verb. (Remember: a complete sentence does not need a direct object, so not all sentences will have them. A sentence needs only a subject and a verb.) When you are looking for a direct object, find the verb and ask *who* or *what.*

Examples:
    I took *the blanket.*
    Jane read *books.*

Indirect Objects
An indirect object is a word or group of words that show how an action had an **influence** on someone or something. If there is an indirect object in a sentence, then you always have a direct object in the sentence. When you are looking for the indirect object, find the verb and ask *to/for whom or what.*

Examples:

We taught [indirect object] the old dog [direct object] a new trick.

I gave [indirect object] them [direct object] a math lesson.

English Conventions
© Mometrix Media - flashcardsecrets.com/louisiana
English I

Discuss subject-verb agreement in the case of compound subjects.

English Conventions
© Mometrix Media - flashcardsecrets.com/louisiana
English I

Discuss subject-verb agreement in the case of indefinite pronouns as the subject, and give examples of indefinite pronouns that are always singular.

English Conventions
© Mometrix Media - flashcardsecrets.com/louisiana
English I

Give examples of subject-verb agreement in cases of indefinite pronouns that are always plural or that depend on the context of the sentence.

English Conventions
© Mometrix Media - flashcardsecrets.com/louisiana
English I

Discuss the following special cases of subject-verb agreement:
plural form and singular meaning
plural form and meaning with no singular equivalent
mathematical operations

English Conventions
© Mometrix Media - flashcardsecrets.com/louisiana
English I

Discuss complements and direct and indirect objects.

Visit *mometrix.com/academy* for a related video.
Enter video code: 817385

English Conventions
© Mometrix Media - flashcardsecrets.com/louisiana
English I

Discuss predicate nominatives and predicate adjectives.

The **subject** of a sentence names who or what the sentence is about. The subject may be directly stated in a sentence, or the subject may be the implied *you*. The **complete subject** includes the simple subject and all of its modifiers. To find the complete subject, ask *Who* or *What* and insert the verb to complete the question. The answer, including any modifiers (adjectives, prepositional phrases, etc.), is the complete subject. To find the **simple subject**, remove all of the modifiers in the complete subject. Being able to locate the subject of a sentence helps with many problems, such as those involving sentence fragments and subject-verb agreement.

Examples:

The small, red <u>car</u> is the one that he wants for Christmas.
(simple subject: car; complete subject: The small, red car)

The young <u>artist</u> is coming over for dinner.
(simple subject: artist; complete subject: The young artist)

In a sentence, you always have a predicate and a subject. The subject tells what the sentence is about, and the **predicate** explains or describes the subject.

Think about the sentence *He sings*. In this sentence, we have a subject (He) and a predicate (sings). This is all that is needed for a sentence to be complete. Most sentences contain more information, but if this is all the information that you are given, then you have a complete sentence.

Now, let's look at another sentence: *John and Jane sing on Tuesday nights at the dance hall.*

subject: John and Jane
predicate: sing on Tuesday nights at the dance hall.

Words that come between the simple subject and the verb have no bearing on subject-verb agreement.

Examples:

The <u>joy</u> of my life <u>returns</u> home tonight.
(singular subject: joy; singular verb: returns)
The phrase *of my life* does not influence the verb *returns*.

The <u>question</u> that still remains unanswered <u>is</u> "Who are you?"
(singular subject: question; singular verb: is)
Don't let the phrase "*that still remains...*" trouble you. The subject *question* goes with *is*.

Interjections are words of exclamation (i.e., audible expression of great feeling) that are used alone or as a part of a sentence. Often, they are used at the beginning of a sentence for an introduction. Sometimes, they can be used in the middle of a sentence to show a change in thought or attitude.

Common Interjections: Hey! | Oh, | Ouch! | Please! | Wow!

In **imperative** sentences, the verb's subject is understood (e.g., [You] Run to the store), but is not actually present in the sentence. Normally, the subject comes before the verb. However, the subject comes after the verb in sentences that begin with *There are* or *There was*.

Direct:
John knows the way to the park.
(Who knows the way to the park? Answer: *John*)
The cookies need ten more minutes.
(What needs ten minutes? Answer: *The cookies*)
By five o'clock, Bill will need to leave.
(Who needs to leave? Answer: *Bill*)

Remember: The subject can come after the verb.
There are five letters on the table for him.
(What is on the table? Answer: *Five letters*)
There were coffee and doughnuts in the house.
(What was in the house? Answer: *Coffee and doughnuts*)

Implied:
Go to the post office for me.
(Who is going to the post office? Answer: *You*.)
Come and sit with me, please?
(Who needs to come and sit? Answer: *You*.)

Verbs **agree** with their subjects in number. In other words, singular subjects need singular verbs. Plural subjects need plural verbs. **Singular** is for **one** person, place, or thing. **Plural** is for **more than one** person, place, or thing. Subjects and verbs must also share the same point of view, as in first, second, or third person. The present tense ending *-s* is used on a verb if its subject is third person singular; otherwise, the verb's ending is not modified.

Number Agreement Examples:

Single Subject and Verb: <u>Dan</u> <u>calls</u> home.
(singular subject: Dan; singular verb: calls)
Dan is one person. So, the singular verb *calls* is needed.

Plural Subject and Verb: <u>Dan and Bob</u> <u>call</u> home.
(plural subject: Dan and Bob; plural verb: call)
More than one person needs the plural verb *call*.

Person Agreement Examples:
First Person: I *am* walking.
Second Person: You *are* walking.
Third Person: He *is* walking.

English Conventions
© Mometrix Media - flashcardsecrets.com/louisiana
English I

Define and discuss interjections.

English Conventions
© Mometrix Media - flashcardsecrets.com/louisiana
English I

Distinguish between the complete subject and the simple subject, and list a few situations in which the subject may be difficult to locate.

Visit *mometrix.com/academy* for a related video.
Enter video code: 444771

English Conventions
© Mometrix Media - flashcardsecrets.com/louisiana
English I

Identify the subject in each of the following sentences:
- John knows the way to the park.
- The cookies need ten more minutes.
- By five o' clock, Bill will need to leave.
- There are five letters on the table for him.
- There were coffee and doughnuts in the house.
- Go to the post office for me.
- Come and sit with me, please?

English Conventions
© Mometrix Media - flashcardsecrets.com/louisiana
English I

Define and discuss predicates.

Visit *mometrix.com/academy* for a related video.
Enter video code: 293942

English Conventions
© Mometrix Media - flashcardsecrets.com/louisiana
English I

Discuss subject-verb agreement.

Visit *mometrix.com/academy* for a related video.
Enter video code: 479190

English Conventions
© Mometrix Media - flashcardsecrets.com/louisiana
English I

Discuss subject-verb agreement in the case of words that come between the subject and the verb.

An **adverb** is a word that is used to **modify** a verb, adjective, or another adverb. Usually, adverbs answer one of these questions: *When? Where? How?* and *Why?* The negatives *not* and *never* are considered adverbs. Adverbs that modify adjectives or other adverbs **strengthen** or **weaken** the words that they modify.

Examples:
> He walks *quickly* through the crowd.
> The water flows *smoothly* on the rocks.

Note: Adverbs are usually indicated by the morpheme *-ly*, which has been added to the root word. For instance, *quick* can be made into an adverb by adding *-ly* to construct *quickly*. Some words that end in *-ly* do not follow this rule and can behave as other parts of speech. Examples of adjectives ending in *-ly* include: *early, friendly, holy, lonely, silly*, and *ugly*. To know if a word that ends in *-ly* is an adjective or adverb, check your dictionary. Also, while many adverbs end in *-ly*, you need to remember that not all adverbs end in *-ly*.

Examples:
> He is *never* angry.
> You are *too* irresponsible to travel alone.

A **preposition** is a word placed before a noun or pronoun that shows the relationship between an object and another word in the sentence.

Common prepositions:

about	before	during	on	under
after	beneath	for	over	until
against	between	from	past	up
among	beyond	in	through	with
around	by	of	to	within
at	down	off	toward	without

Examples:
> The napkin is *in* the drawer.
> The Earth rotates *around* the Sun.
> The needle is *beneath* the haystack.
> Can you find "me" *among* the words?

Common subordinating conjunctions include:

after	since	whenever
although	so that	where
because	unless	wherever
before	until	whether
in order that	when	while

Examples:
> I am hungry *because* I did not eat breakfast.
> He went home *when* everyone left.

Some adjectives are relative and other adjectives are absolute. Adjectives that are **relative** can show the comparison between things. **Absolute** adjectives can also show comparison, but they do so in a different way. Let's say that you are reading two books. You think that one book is perfect, and the other book is not exactly perfect. It is not possible for one book to be more perfect than the other. Either you think that the book is perfect, or you think that the book is imperfect. In this case, perfect and imperfect are absolute adjectives.

Relative adjectives will show the different **degrees** of something or someone to something else or someone else. The three degrees of adjectives include positive, comparative, and superlative.

The **positive** degree is the normal form of an adjective.
> Example: This work is *difficult*. | She is *smart*.

The **comparative** degree compares one person or thing to another person or thing.
> Example: This work is *more difficult* than your work. | She is *smarter* than me.

The **superlative** degree compares more than two people or things.
> Example: This is the *most difficult* work of my life. | She is the *smartest* lady in school.

The rules for comparing adverbs are the same as the rules for adjectives.

The **positive** degree is the standard form of an adverb.
> Example: He arrives *soon*. | She speaks *softly* to her friends.

The **comparative** degree compares one person or thing to another person or thing.
> Example: He arrives *sooner* than Sarah. | She speaks *more softly* than him.

The **superlative** degree compares more than two people or things.
> Example: He arrives *soonest* of the group. | She speaks the *most softly* of any of her friends.

Conjunctions join words, phrases, or clauses and they show the connection between the joined pieces. **Coordinating conjunctions** connect equal parts of sentences. **Correlative conjunctions** show the connection between pairs. **Subordinating conjunctions** join subordinate (i.e., dependent) clauses with independent clauses.

The **coordinating conjunctions** include: *and, but, yet, or, nor, for,* and *so*

Examples:
> The rock was small, *but* it was heavy.
> She drove in the night, *and* he drove in the day.

The **correlative conjunctions** are: *either…or* | *neither…nor* | *not only…but also*

Examples:
> *Either* you are coming *or* you are staying.
> He *not only* ran three miles *but also* swam 200 yards.

English Conventions
© Mometrix Media - flashcardsecrets.com/louisiana
English I

Describe relative and absolute adjectives.

Visit *mometrix.com/academy* for a related video.
Enter video code: 470154

English Conventions
© Mometrix Media - flashcardsecrets.com/louisiana
English I

Define and discuss adverbs.

English Conventions
© Mometrix Media - flashcardsecrets.com/louisiana
English I

Describe the rules for comparing adverbs and adjectives.

Visit *mometrix.com/academy* for related videos.
Enter video codes: 713951 and 400865

English Conventions
© Mometrix Media - flashcardsecrets.com/louisiana
English I

Describe prepositions and how they are used.

Visit *mometrix.com/academy* for a related video.
Enter video code: 946763

English Conventions
© Mometrix Media - flashcardsecrets.com/louisiana
English I

Describe conjunctions and how they are used.

Visit *mometrix.com/academy* for a related video.
Enter video code: 390329

English Conventions
© Mometrix Media - flashcardsecrets.com/louisiana
English I

Discuss common subordinating conjunctions.

Visit *mometrix.com/academy* for a related video.
Enter video code: 958913

Present perfect: The action started in the past and continues into the present or took place previously at an unspecified time
    Example: I *have walked* to the store three times today.

Past perfect: The second action happened in the past. The first action came before the second.
    Example: Before I walked to the store (Action 2), I *had walked* to the library (Action 1).

Future perfect: An action that uses the past and the future. In other words, the action is complete before a future moment.
    Example: When she comes for the supplies (future moment), I *will have walked* to the store (action completed before the future moment).

A verb **tense** shows the different form of a verb to point to the time of an action. The present and past tense are indicated by the verb's form. An action in the present, *I talk,* can change form for the past: *I talked.* However, for the other tenses, an auxiliary (i.e., helping) verb is needed to show the change in form. These helping verbs include *am, are, is | have, has, had | was, were, will* (or *shall*).

Present: I talk	Present perfect: I have talked
Past: I talked	Past perfect: I had talked
Future: I will talk	Future perfect: I will have talked

Present: The action happens at the current time.
    Example: He *walks* to the store every morning.

To show that something is happening right now, use the progressive present tense: I *am walking.*

Past: The action happened in the past.
    Example: He *walked* to the store an hour ago.

Future: The action is going to happen later.
    Example: I *will walk* to the store tomorrow.

There are three **moods** in English: the indicative, the imperative, and the subjunctive.

The **indicative mood** is used for facts, opinions, and questions.
    Fact: You can do this.
    Opinion: I think that you can do this.
    Question: Do you know that you can do this?

The **imperative** is used for orders or requests.
    Order: You are going to do this!
    Request: Will you do this for me?

The **subjunctive mood** is for wishes and statements that go against fact.
    Wish: I wish that I were famous.
    Statement against fact: If I were you, I would do this. (This goes against fact because I am not you. You have the chance to do this, and I do not have the chance.)

When you need to change the form of a verb, you are **conjugating** a verb. The key forms of a verb are singular, present tense (dream); singular, past tense (dreamed); and the past participle (have dreamed). Note: the past participle needs a helping verb to make a verb tense. For example, I *have dreamed* of this day. The following tables demonstrate some of the different ways to conjugate a verb:

Singular

Tense	First Person	Second Person	Third Person
Present	I dream	You dream	He, she, it dreams
Past	I dreamed	You dreamed	He, she, it dreamed
Past Participle	I have dreamed	You have dreamed	He, she, it has dreamed

Plural

Tense	First Person	Second Person	Third Person
Present	We dream	You dream	They dream
Past	We dreamed	You dreamed	They dreamed
Past Participle	We have dreamed	You have dreamed	They have dreamed

Articles are adjectives that are used to distinguish nouns as definite or indefinite. **Definite** nouns are preceded by the article *the* and indicate a specific person, place, thing, or idea. **Indefinite** nouns are preceded by *a* or *an* and do not indicate a specific person, place, thing, or idea. *A, an,* and *the* are the only articles. Note: *An* comes before words that start with a vowel sound. For example, "Are you going to get an umbrella?"

    Definite: I lost *the* bottle that belongs to me.
    Indefinite: Does anyone have *a* bottle to share?

An **adjective** is a word that is used to modify a noun or pronoun. An adjective answers a question: *Which one? What kind?* or *How many?* Usually, adjectives come before the words that they modify, but they may also come after a linking verb.

    Which one? The *third* suit is my favorite.
    What kind? This suit is *navy blue.*
    How many? I am going to buy *four* pairs of socks to match the suit.

English Conventions
© Mometrix Media - flashcardsecrets.com/louisiana
English I

Discuss verb tenses.

English Conventions
© Mometrix Media - flashcardsecrets.com/louisiana
English I

Discuss perfect verb tenses.

English Conventions
© Mometrix Media - flashcardsecrets.com/louisiana
English I

Describe the process of conjugating verbs.

English Conventions
© Mometrix Media - flashcardsecrets.com/louisiana
English I

Discuss indicative, imperative, and subjunctive moods.

Visit *mometrix.com/academy* for a related video.
Enter video code: 269472

English Conventions
© Mometrix Media - flashcardsecrets.com/louisiana
English I

Define adjectives and discuss their function.

English Conventions
© Mometrix Media - flashcardsecrets.com/louisiana
English I

Define and discuss articles.

Pronouns are words that are used to stand in for nouns. A pronoun may be classified as personal, intensive, relative, interrogative, demonstrative, indefinite, and reciprocal.

Personal: *Nominative* is the case for nouns and pronouns that are the subject of a sentence. *Objective* is the case for nouns and pronouns that are an object in a sentence. *Possessive* is the case for nouns and pronouns that show possession or ownership.

Singular

	Nominative	Objective	Possessive
First Person	I	me	my, mine
Second Person	you	you	your, yours
Third Person	he, she, it	him, her, it	his, her, hers, its

Plural

	Nominative	Objective	Possessive
First Person	we	us	our, ours
Second Person	you	you	your, yours
Third Person	they	them	their, theirs

Collective nouns are the names for a group of people, places, or things that may act as a whole. The following are examples of collective nouns: *class, company, dozen, group, herd, team,* and *public*. Collective nouns usually require an article, which denotes the noun as being a single unit. For instance, a choir is a group of singers. Even though there are many singers in a choir, the word choir is grammatically treated as a single unit. If we refer to the members of the group, and not the group itself, it is no longer a collective noun.

    Incorrect: The *choir are* going to compete nationally this year.
    Correct: The *choir is* going to compete nationally this year.
    Incorrect: The *members* of the choir *is* competing nationally this year.
    Correct: The *members* of the choir *are* competing nationally this year.

If you want to write a sentence, then you need a verb. Without a verb, you have no sentence. The verb of a sentence indicates action or being. In other words, the verb shows something's action or state of being or the action that has been done to something.

A **transitive verb** is a verb whose action (e.g., drive, run, jump) indicates a receiver (e.g., car, dog, kangaroo). **Intransitive verbs** do not indicate a receiver of an action. In other words, the action of the verb does not point to a subject or object.

    Transitive: He plays the piano. | The piano was played by him.
    Intransitive: He plays. | John plays well.

A dictionary will tell you whether a verb is transitive or intransitive. Some verbs can be transitive and intransitive.

Intensive: I myself, you yourself, he himself, she herself, the (thing) itself, we ourselves, you yourselves, they themselves

Relative: which, who, whom, whose

Interrogative: what, which, who, whom, whose

Demonstrative: this, that, these, those

Indefinite: all, any, each, everyone, either/neither, one, some, several

Reciprocal: each other, one another

Transitive verbs come in active or passive **voice**. If something does an action or is acted upon, then you will know whether a verb is active or passive. When the subject of the sentence is doing the action, the verb is in **active voice**. When the subject is acted upon, the verb is in **passive voice**.

    Active: Jon drew the picture. (The subject *Jon* is doing the action of *drawing a picture*.)
    Passive: The picture is drawn by Jon. (The subject *picture* is receiving the action from Jon.)

Action verbs show what the subject is doing. In other words, an action verb shows action. Unlike most types of words, a single action verb, in the right context, can be an entire sentence. **Linking verbs** link the subject of a sentence to a noun or pronoun, or they link a subject with an adjective. You always need a verb if you want a complete sentence. However, linking verbs on their own cannot be a complete sentence. Common linking verbs include *appear, be, become, feel, grow, look, seem, smell, sound,* and *taste*. However, any verb that shows a condition and connects to a noun, pronoun, or adjective that describes the subject of a sentence is a linking verb.

Action: He sings. | Run! | Go! | I talk with him every day. | She reads.

Linking:
    Incorrect: I am.
    Correct: I am John. | I smell roses. | I feel tired.

Note: Some verbs are followed by words that look like prepositions, but they are a part of the verb and a part of the verb's meaning. These are known as phrasal verbs, and examples include *call off, look up,* and *drop off*.

English Conventions
© Mometrix Media - flashcardsecrets.com/louisiana
English I

Define collective nouns.

English Conventions
© Mometrix Media - flashcardsecrets.com/louisiana
English I

Describe pronouns and their use, and discuss personal pronouns in particular.

English Conventions
© Mometrix Media - flashcardsecrets.com/louisiana
English I

Discuss how pronouns can be grouped.

Visit *mometrix.com/academy* for a related video.
Enter video code: 312073

English Conventions
© Mometrix Media - flashcardsecrets.com/louisiana
English I

Describe transitive and intransitive verbs and discuss their uses.

English Conventions
© Mometrix Media - flashcardsecrets.com/louisiana
English I

Describe action verbs and linking verbs.

Visit *mometrix.com/academy* for a related video.
Enter video code: 743142

English Conventions
© Mometrix Media - flashcardsecrets.com/louisiana
English I

Discuss transitive verbs with active and passive voice.

Like unknown words, the meanings of phrases, paragraphs, and entire works can also be difficult to discern. Each of these can be better understood with added context. However, for larger groups of words, more context is needed. Unclear phrases are similar to unclear words, and the same methods can be used to understand their meaning. However, it is also important to consider how the individual words in the phrase work together. Paragraphs are a bit more complicated. Just as words must be compared to other words in a sentence, paragraphs must be compared to other paragraphs in a composition or a section.

The syntax, or structure, of a sentence affords grammatical cues that aid readers in comprehending the meanings of words, phrases, and sentences in the texts that they read. Seemingly minor differences in how the words or phrases in a sentence are ordered can make major differences in meaning. For example, two sentences can use exactly the same words but have different meanings based on the word order:
- "The man with a broken arm sat in a chair.
- "The man sat in a chair with a broken arm."

While both sentences indicate that a man sat in a chair, differing syntax indicates whether the man's or chair's arm was broken.

While these strategies are useful for determining the meaning of unknown words and phrases, sometimes additional resources are needed to properly use the terms in different contexts. Some words have multiple definitions, and some words are inappropriate in particular contexts or modes of writing. The following tools are helpful for understanding all meanings and proper uses for words and phrases.
- **Dictionaries** provide the meaning of a multitude of words in a language. Many dictionaries include additional information about each word, such as its etymology, its synonyms, or variations of the word.
- **Glossaries** are similar to dictionaries, as they provide the meanings of a variety of terms. However, while dictionaries typically feature an extensive list of words and comprise an entire publication, glossaries are often included at the end of a text and only include terms and definitions that are relevant to the text they follow.
- **Spell Checkers** are used to detect spelling errors in typed text. Some spell checkers may also detect the misuse of plural or singular nouns, verb tenses, or capitalization. While spell checkers are a helpful tool, they are not always reliable or attuned to the author's intent, so it is important to review the spell checker's suggestions before accepting them.
- **Style Manuals** are guidelines on the preferred punctuation, format, and grammar usage according to different fields or organizations. For example, the Associated Press Stylebook is a style guide often used for media writing. The guidelines within a style guide are not always applicable across different contexts and usages, as the guidelines often cover grammatical or formatting situations that are not objectively correct or incorrect.

To understand the meaning of an entire composition, the type of composition must be considered. **Expository writing** is generally organized so that each paragraph focuses on explaining one idea, or part of an idea, and its relevance. **Persuasive writing** uses paragraphs for different purposes to organize the parts of the argument. **Unclear paragraphs** must be read in the context of the paragraphs around them for their meaning to be fully understood. The meaning of full texts can also be unclear at times. The purpose of composition is also important for understanding the meaning of a text. To quickly understand the broad meaning of a text, look to the introductory and concluding paragraphs. Fictional texts are different. Some fictional works have implicit meanings, but some do not. The target audience must be considered for understanding texts that do have an implicit meaning, as most children's fiction will clearly state any lessons or morals. For other fiction, the application of literary theories and criticism may be helpful for understanding the text.

General nouns are the names of conditions or ideas. **Specific nouns** name people, places, and things that are understood by using your senses.

General nouns:
    Condition: beauty, strength
    Idea: truth, peace

Specific nouns:
    People: baby, friend, father
    Places: town, park, city hall
    Things: rainbow, cough, apple, silk, gasoline

When you talk about a person, place, thing, or idea, you are talking about a noun. The two main types of nouns are common and proper nouns. Also, nouns can be abstract (i.e., general) or concrete (i.e., specific).

Common nouns are generic names for people, places, and thing. Common nouns are not usually capitalized. Examples of common nouns:
    People: boy, girl, worker, manager
    Places: school, bank, library, home
    Things: dog, cat, truck, car

Proper nouns name specific people, places, or things. All proper nouns are capitalized. Examples of proper nouns:
    People: Abraham Lincoln; George Washington; Martin Luther King, Jr.
    Places: Los Angeles, California; New York; Asia
    Things: Statue of Liberty, Earth*, Lincoln Memorial

Note: When referring to the planet that we live on, capitalize *Earth*. When referring to the dirt, rocks, or land, lowercase *earth*.

English Conventions
© Mometrix Media - flashcardsecrets.com/louisiana
English I

Describe how syntax can affect clarity and meaning.

Visit *mometrix.com/academy* for a related video.
Enter video code: 242280

English Conventions
© Mometrix Media - flashcardsecrets.com/louisiana
English I

Discuss considerations for determining the meaning of phrases and paragraphs.

English Conventions
© Mometrix Media - flashcardsecrets.com/louisiana
English I

Discuss how the type and purpose of a composition affects the meaning of the composition.

English Conventions
© Mometrix Media - flashcardsecrets.com/louisiana
English I

List and define tools for determining the meaning and proper usage of unknown words and phrases.

English Conventions
© Mometrix Media - flashcardsecrets.com/louisiana
English I

Define common nouns and proper nouns.

English Conventions
© Mometrix Media - flashcardsecrets.com/louisiana
English I

Define general nouns and specific nouns.

An author may use a word and then give examples that illustrate its meaning. Consider this text: "Teachers who do not know how to use sign language can help students who are deaf or hard of hearing understand certain instructions by using gestures instead, like pointing their fingers to indicate which direction to look or go; holding up a hand, palm outward, to indicate stopping; holding the hands flat, palms up, curling a finger toward oneself in a beckoning motion to indicate 'come here'; or curling all fingers toward oneself repeatedly to indicate 'come on', 'more', or 'continue.'" The author of this text has used the word "gestures" and then followed it with examples, so a reader unfamiliar with the word could deduce from the examples that "gestures" means "hand motions." Readers can find examples by looking for signal words "for example," "for instance," "like," "such as," and "e.g.."

If readers simply bypass unknown words, they can reach unclear conclusions about what they read. However, looking for the definition of every unfamiliar word in the dictionary can slow their reading progress. Moreover, the dictionary may list multiple definitions for a word, so readers must search the word's context for meaning. Hence context is important to new vocabulary regardless of reader methods. Four types of context clues are examples, definitions, descriptive words, and opposites. Authors may use a certain word, and then follow it with several different examples of what it describes. Sometimes authors actually supply a definition of a word they use, which is especially true in informational and technical texts. Authors may use descriptive words that elaborate upon a vocabulary word they just used. Authors may also use opposites with negation that help define meaning.

When readers encounter a word they do not recognize in a text, the author may expand on that word to illustrate it better. While the author may do this to make the prose more picturesque and vivid, the reader can also take advantage of this description to provide context clues to the meaning of the unfamiliar word. For example, an author may write, "The man sitting next to me on the airplane was obese. His shirt stretched across his vast expanse of flesh, strained almost to bursting." The descriptive second sentence elaborates on and helps to define the previous sentence's word 'obese' to mean extremely fat. A reader unfamiliar with the word "repugnant" can decipher its meaning through an author's accompanying description: "The way the child grimaced and shuddered as he swallowed the medicine showed that its taste was particularly repugnant."

While readers sometimes have to look for definitions of unfamiliar words in a dictionary or do some work to determine a word's meaning from its surrounding context, at other times an author may make it easier for readers by defining certain words. For example, an author may write, "The company did not have sufficient capital, that is, available money, to continue operations." The author defined "capital" as "available money," and heralded the definition with the phrase "that is." Another way that authors supply word definitions is with appositives. Rather than being introduced by a signal phrase like "that is," "namely," or "meaning," an appositive comes after the vocabulary word it defines and is enclosed within two commas. For example, an author may write, "The Indians introduced the Pilgrims to pemmican, cakes they made of lean meat dried and mixed with fat, which proved greatly beneficial to keep settlers from starving while trapping." In this example, the appositive phrase following "pemmican" and preceding "which" defines the word "pemmican."

Syntax refers to sentence structure and word order. Suppose that a reader encounters an unfamiliar word when reading a text. To illustrate, consider an invented word like "splunch." If this word is used in a sentence like "Please splunch that ball to me," the reader can assume from syntactic context that "splunch" is a verb. We would not use a noun, adjective, adverb, or preposition with the object "that ball," and the prepositional phrase "to me" further indicates "splunch" represents an action. However, in the sentence, "Please hand that splunch to me," the reader can assume that "splunch" is a noun. Demonstrative adjectives like "that" modify nouns. Also, we hand someone some*thing*—a thing being a noun; we do not hand someone a verb, adjective, or adverb. Some sentences contain further clues. For example, from the sentence, "The princess wore the glittering splunch on her head," the reader can deduce that it is a crown, tiara, or something similar from the syntactic context, without knowing the word.

Text authors sometimes introduce a contrasting or opposing idea before or after a concept they present. They may do this to emphasize or heighten the idea they present by contrasting it with something that is the reverse. However, readers can also use these context clues to understand familiar words. For example, an author may write, "Our conversation was not cheery. We sat and talked very solemnly about his experience and a number of similar events." The reader who is not familiar with the word "solemnly" can deduce by the author's preceding use of "not cheery" that "solemn" means the opposite of cheery or happy, so it must mean serious or sad. Or if someone writes, "Don't condemn his entire project because you couldn't find anything good to say about it," readers unfamiliar with "condemn" can understand from the sentence structure that it means the opposite of saying anything good, so it must mean reject, dismiss, or disapprove. "Entire" adds another context clue, meaning total or complete rejection.

English Conventions
© Mometrix Media - flashcardsecrets.com/louisiana
English I

Give some reasons that using context clues to help determine the meanings of unfamiliar vocabulary can improve reading comprehension. Identify and define four types of context clues.

English Conventions
© Mometrix Media - flashcardsecrets.com/louisiana
English I

Use some text to explain how an author may use examples of a vocabulary word that readers can use to help them deduce its meaning, and describe how readers can more easily locate such examples.

English Conventions
© Mometrix Media - flashcardsecrets.com/louisiana
English I

Explain, including examples, how authors use definitions, including appositives, that can help readers determine the meanings of vocabulary words they do not know in a text.

English Conventions
© Mometrix Media - flashcardsecrets.com/louisiana
English I

Using related descriptions that readers can use as context clues to help them comprehend the meanings of unfamiliar vocabulary words.

English Conventions
© Mometrix Media - flashcardsecrets.com/louisiana
English I

Using examples, explain how authors may use related descriptions that readers can use as context clues to help them comprehend the meanings of unfamiliar vocabulary words.

English Conventions
© Mometrix Media - flashcardsecrets.com/louisiana
English I

Give some examples of how a reader can use the syntax of a sentence to determine which part of speech an unfamiliar word is, and sometimes also to approximate the meaning of the word.

Readers of all levels will encounter words that they have either never seen or have encountered only on a limited basis. The best way to define a word in **context** is to look for nearby words that can assist in revealing the meaning of the word. For instance, unfamiliar nouns are often accompanied by examples that provide a definition. Consider the following sentence: *Dave arrived at the party in hilarious garb: a leopard-print shirt, buckskin trousers, and bright green sneakers.* If a reader was unfamiliar with the meaning of garb, he or she could read the examples (i.e., a leopard-print shirt, buckskin trousers, and bright green sneakers) and quickly determine that the word means *clothing*. Examples will not always be this obvious. Consider this sentence: *Parsley, lemon, and flowers were just a few of the items he used as garnishes.* Here, the word *garnishes* is exemplified by parsley, lemon, and flowers. Readers who have eaten in a variety of restaurants will probably be able to identify a garnish as something used to decorate a plate.

A word's denotation is simply its objective dictionary definition. However, its connotation refers to the subjective associations, often emotional, that specific words evoke in listeners and readers. Two or more words can have the same dictionary meaning, but very different connotations. Writers use diction (word choice) to convey various nuances of thought and emotion by selecting synonyms for other words that best communicate the associations they want to trigger for readers. For example, a car engine is naturally greasy; in this sense, "greasy" is a neutral term. But when a person's smile, appearance, or clothing is described as "greasy," it has a negative connotation. Some words have even gained additional or different meanings over time. For example, *awful* used to be used to describe things that evoked a sense of awe. When *awful* is separated into its root word, awe, and suffix, -ful, it can be understood to mean "full of awe." However, the word is now commonly used to describe things that evoke repulsion, terror, or another intense, negative reaction.

In some cases, there will be very few contextual clues to help a reader define the meaning of an unfamiliar word. When this happens, one strategy that readers may employ is **substitution**. A good reader will brainstorm some possible synonyms for the given word, and he or she will substitute these words into the sentence. If the sentence and the surrounding passage continue to make sense, then the substitution has revealed at least some information about the unfamiliar word. Consider the sentence: *Frank's admonition rang in her ears as she climbed the mountain.* A reader unfamiliar with *admonition* might come up with some substitutions like *vow, promise, advice, complaint,* or *compliment.* All of these words make general sense of the sentence, though their meanings are diverse. However, this process has suggested that an admonition is some sort of message. The substitution strategy is rarely able to pinpoint a precise definition, but this process can be effective as a last resort.

In addition to looking at the context of a passage, readers can use contrast to define an unfamiliar word in context. In many sentences, the author will not describe the unfamiliar word directly; instead, he or she will describe the opposite of the unfamiliar word. Thus, you are provided with some information that will bring you closer to defining the word. Consider the following example: *Despite his intelligence, Hector's low brow and bad posture made him look obtuse.* The author writes that Hector's appearance does not convey intelligence. Therefore, *obtuse* must mean unintelligent. Here is another example: *Despite the horrible weather, we were beatific about our trip to Alaska.* The word *despite* indicates that the speaker's feelings were at odds with the weather. Since the weather is described as *horrible*, then *beatific* must mean something positive.

When a word has more than one meaning, readers can have difficulty determining how the word is being used in a given sentence. For instance, the verb *cleave,* can mean either *join* or *separate.* When readers come upon this word, they will have to select the definition that makes the most sense. Consider the following sentence: *Hermione's knife cleaved the bread cleanly.* Since a knife cannot join bread together, the word must indicate separation. A slightly more difficult example would be the sentence: *The birds cleaved to one another as they flew from the oak tree.* Immediately, the presence of the words *to one another* should suggest that in this sentence *cleave* is being used to mean *join.* Discovering the intent of a word with multiple meanings requires the same tricks as defining an unknown word: look for contextual clues and evaluate the substituted words.

Occasionally, you will be able to define an unfamiliar word by looking at the descriptive words in the context. Consider the following sentence: *Fred dragged the recalcitrant boy kicking and screaming up the stairs.* The words *dragged, kicking,* and *screaming* all suggest that the boy does not want to go up the stairs. The reader may assume that *recalcitrant* means something like unwilling or protesting. In this example, an unfamiliar adjective was identified.

Additionally, using description to define an unfamiliar noun is a common practice compared to unfamiliar adjectives, as in this sentence: *Don's wrinkled frown and constantly shaking fist identified him as a curmudgeon of the first order.* Don is described as having a *wrinkled frown and constantly shaking fist*, suggesting that a *curmudgeon* must be a grumpy person. Contrasts do not always provide detailed information about the unfamiliar word, but they at least give the reader some clues.

English Conventions
© Mometrix Media - flashcardsecrets.com/louisiana
English I

Discuss nuances of word meaning relative to connotation versus denotation, diction, and usage. Give some examples of words whose meanings have acquired additional or different connotations over time because of popular usage.

English Conventions
© Mometrix Media - flashcardsecrets.com/louisiana
English I

Discuss how to define a word in context.

English Conventions
© Mometrix Media - flashcardsecrets.com/louisiana
English I

Discuss how contrasts can be used to define a word in context.

English Conventions
© Mometrix Media - flashcardsecrets.com/louisiana
English I

Describe the use of substitution for identifying the meaning of uncommon words in context.

English Conventions
© Mometrix Media - flashcardsecrets.com/louisiana
English I

Discuss how descriptions can be used to define a word in context.

English Conventions
© Mometrix Media - flashcardsecrets.com/louisiana
English I

Describe the process for determining the contextual meaning of a word with multiple definitions.

Adjective Suffixes

Suffix	Definition	Examples
-able (-ible)	capable of being	toler*able*, ed*ible*
-esque	in the style of, like	picturesque, grotesque
-ful	filled with, marked by	thankful, zestful
-ic	make, cause	terrific, beatific
-ish	suggesting, like	churlish, childish
-less	lacking, without	hopeless, countless
-ous	marked by, given to	religious, riotous

Miscellaneous Prefixes

Prefix	Definition	Examples
neo-	new	Neolithic, neoconservative
omni-	all, everywhere	omniscient, omnivore
ortho-	right, straight	orthogonal, orthodox
over-	above	overbearing, oversight
pan-	all, entire	panorama, pandemonium
para-	beside, beyond	parallel, paradox
phil-	love, like	philosophy, philanthropic
prim-	first, early	primitive, primary
re-	backward, again	revoke, recur
sym-	with, together	sympathy, symphony
vis-	to see	visage, visible

Noun Suffixes

Suffix	Definition	Examples
-ism	act, manner, doctrine	barbarism, socialism
-ist	worker, follower	monopolist, socialist
-ity (-ty)	state, quality, condition	acid*ity*, civil*ity*, royal*ty*
-ment	result, action	refreshment, disappointment
-ness	quality, state	greatness, tallness
-ship	position	internship, statesmanship
-sion (-tion)	state, result	re*vision*, expedi*tion*
-th	act, state, quality	warmth, width
-tude	quality, state, result	magnitude, fortitude

Noun Suffixes

Suffix	Definition	Examples
-acy	state, condition	accuracy, privacy
-ance	act, condition, fact	acceptance, vigilance
-ard	one that does excessively	drunkard, sluggard
-ation	action, state, result	occupation, starvation
-dom	state, rank, condition	serfdom, wisdom
-er (-or)	office, action	teach*er*, elevat*or*, hon*or*
-ess	feminine	waitress, duchess
-hood	state, condition	manhood, statehood
-ion	action, result, state	union, fusion

The **denotative** meaning of a word is the literal meaning. The **connotative** meaning goes beyond the denotative meaning to include the emotional reaction that a word may invoke. The connotative meaning often takes the denotative meaning a step further due to associations the reader makes with the denotative meaning. Readers can differentiate between the denotative and connotative meanings by first recognizing how authors use each meaning. Most non-fiction, for example, is fact-based and authors do not use flowery, figurative language. The reader can assume that the writer is using the denotative meaning of words. In fiction, the author may use the connotative meaning. Readers can determine whether the author is using the denotative or connotative meaning of a word by implementing context clues.

Verb Suffixes

Suffix	Definition	Examples
-ate	having, showing	separate, desolate
-en	cause to be, become	deepen, strengthen
-fy	make, cause to have	glorify, fortify
-ize	cause to be, treat with	sterilize, mechanize, criticize

English Conventions
© Mometrix Media - flashcardsecrets.com/louisiana
English I

Define and give examples of the following prefixes: neo-, omni-, ortho-, over-, pan-, para-, phil-, prim-, re-, sym-, and vis-.

English Conventions
© Mometrix Media - flashcardsecrets.com/louisiana
English I

Define and give examples of the following suffixes: -able (-ible), -esque, -ful, -ic, -ish, -less, and -ous.

English Conventions
© Mometrix Media - flashcardsecrets.com/louisiana
English I

Define and give examples of the following suffixes: -acy, -ance, -ard, ation, -dom, -er(-or), -ess, -hood, and -ion.

English Conventions
© Mometrix Media - flashcardsecrets.com/louisiana
English I

Define and give examples of the following suffixes: -ism, -ist, -ity(-ty), -ment, -ness, -ship, -sion(-tion), -th, and -tude.

English Conventions
© Mometrix Media - flashcardsecrets.com/louisiana
English I

Define and give examples of the following suffixes: -ate, -en, fy, and -ize.

English Conventions
© Mometrix Media - flashcardsecrets.com/louisiana
English I

Discuss how to differentiate between the connotative and denotative meanings of words.

Time and Space Prefixes

Prefix	Definition	Examples
a-	in, on, of, up, to	abed, afoot
ab-	from, away, off	abdicate, abjure
ad-	to, toward	advance, adventure
ante-	before, previous	antecedent, antedate
anti-	against, opposing	antipathy, antidote
cata-	down, away, thoroughly	catastrophe, cataclysm
circum-	around	circumspect, circumference
com-	with, together, very	commotion, complicate
contra-	against, opposing	contradict, contravene
de-	from	depart

Amount

Prefix	Definition	Examples
bi-	two	bisect, biennial
mono-	one, single	monogamy, monologue
poly-	many	polymorphous, polygamous
semi-	half, partly	semicircle, semicolon
uni-	one	uniform, unity

Time and Space Prefixes

Prefix	Definition	Examples
post-	after, following	postpone, postscript
pre-	before, previous	prevent, preclude
pro-	forward, in place of	propel, pronoun
retro-	back, backward	retrospect, retrograde
sub-	under, beneath	subjugate, substitute
super-	above, extra	supersede, supernumerary
trans-	across, beyond, over	transact, transport

Time and Space Prefixes

Prefix	Definition	Examples
dia-	through, across, apart	diameter, diagnose
dis-	away, off, down, not	dissent, disappear
epi-	upon	epilogue
ex-	out	extract, excerpt
hypo-	under, beneath	hypodermic, hypothesis
inter-	among, between	intercede, interrupt
intra-	within	intramural, intrastate
ob-	against, opposing	objection
per-	through	perceive, permit
peri-	around	periscope, perimeter

Miscellaneous Prefixes

Prefix	Definition	Examples
equi-	equal	equivalent, equilibrium
for-	away, off, from	forget, forswear
fore-	previous	foretell, forefathers
homo-	same, equal	homogenized, homonym
hyper-	excessive, over	hypercritical, hypertension
in-	in, into	intrude, invade
mal-	bad, poorly, not	malfunction, malpractice
mis-	bad, poorly, not	misspell, misfire
mor-	death	mortality, mortuary

Negation

Prefix	Definition	Examples
a-	without, lacking	atheist, agnostic
in-	not, opposing	incapable, ineligible
non-	not	nonentity, nonsense
un-	not, reverse of	unhappy, unlock

English Conventions
© Mometrix Media - flashcardsecrets.com/louisiana
English I

Define and give examples of the following prefixes: bi-, mono-, poly-, semi-, and uni-.

English Conventions
© Mometrix Media - flashcardsecrets.com/louisiana
English I

Define and give examples of the following prefixes: a-, ab-, ad-, ante-, anti-, cata-, circum-, com-, contra-, and de-.

English Conventions
© Mometrix Media - flashcardsecrets.com/louisiana
English I

Define and give examples of the following prefixes: dia-, dis-, epi-, ex-, hypo-, inter-, intra-, ob-, per-, and peri-.

English Conventions
© Mometrix Media - flashcardsecrets.com/louisiana
English I

Define and give examples of the following prefixes: post-, pre-, pro-, retro-, sub-, super-, and trans-.

English Conventions
© Mometrix Media - flashcardsecrets.com/louisiana
English I

Define and give examples of the following prefixes: a-, in-, non-, and un-.

English Conventions
© Mometrix Media - flashcardsecrets.com/louisiana
English I

Define and give examples of the following prefixes: belli-, bene-, equi-, for-, fore-, homo-, hyper-, in-, magn-, mal-, mis-, and mor-.

Antonyms are words with opposite meanings. *Light* and *dark*, *up* and *down*, *right* and *left*, *good* and *bad*: these are all sets of antonyms. Be careful to distinguish between antonyms and pairs of words that are simply different. *Black* and *gray*, for instance, are not antonyms because gray is not the opposite of black. *Black* and *white*, on the other hand, are antonyms.

Not every word has an antonym. For instance, many nouns do not. What would be the antonym of *chair*? During your exam, the questions related to antonyms are more likely to concern adjectives. You will recall that adjectives are words that describe a noun. Some common adjectives include *purple*, *fast*, *skinny*, and *sweet*. From those four adjectives, *purple* is the item that lacks a group of obvious antonyms.

When you understand how words relate to each other, you will discover more in a passage. This is explained by understanding **synonyms** (e.g., words that mean the same thing) and **antonyms** (e.g., words that mean the opposite of one another). As an example, *dry* and *arid* are synonyms, and *dry* and *wet* are antonyms.

There are many pairs of words in English that can be considered synonyms, despite having slightly different definitions. For instance, the words *friendly* and *collegial* can both be used to describe a warm interpersonal relationship, and one would be correct to call them synonyms. However, *collegial* (kin to *colleague*) is often used in reference to professional or academic relationships, and *friendly* has no such connotation.

If the difference between the two words is too great, then they should not be called synonyms. *Hot* and *warm* are not synonyms because their meanings are too distinct. A good way to determine whether two words are synonyms is to substitute one word for the other word and verify that the meaning of the sentence has not changed. Substituting *warm* for *hot* in a sentence would convey a different meaning. Although warm and hot may seem close in meaning, warm generally means that the temperature is moderate, and hot generally means that the temperature is excessively high.

Many English words were formed from combining multiple sources. For example, the Latin *habēre* means "to have," and the prefixes *in-* and *im-* mean a lack or prevention of something, as in *insufficient* and *imperfect*. Latin combined *in-* with *habēre* to form *inhibēre,* whose past participle was *inhibitus.* This is the origin of the English word *inhibit,* meaning to prevent from having. Hence by knowing the meanings of both the prefix and the root, one can decipher the word meaning. In Greek, the root *enkephalo-* refers to the brain. Many medical terms are based on this root, such as encephalitis and hydrocephalus. Understanding the prefix and suffix meanings (*-itis* means inflammation; *hydro-* means water) allows a person to deduce that encephalitis refers to brain inflammation and hydrocephalus refers to water (or other fluid) in the brain.

Affixes in the English language are morphemes that are added to words to create related but different words. Derivational affixes form new words based on and related to the original words. For example, the affix *–ness* added to the end of the adjective *happy* forms the noun *happiness.* Inflectional affixes form different grammatical versions of words. For example, the plural affix *–s* changes the singular noun *book* to the plural noun *books*, and the past tense affix *–ed* changes the present tense verb *look* to the past tense *looked.* Prefixes are affixes placed in front of words. For example, *heat* means to make hot; *preheat* means to heat in advance. Suffixes are affixes placed at the ends of words. The *happiness* example above contains the suffix *–ness.* Circumfixes add parts both before and after words, such as how *light* becomes *enlighten* with the prefix *en-* and the suffix *–en.* Interfixes create compound words via central affixes: *speed* and *meter* become *speedometer* via the interfix *–o–*.

In English, certain suffixes generally indicate both that a word is a noun, and that the noun represents a state of being or quality. For example, *-ness* is commonly used to change an adjective into its noun form, as with *happy* and *happiness, nice* and *niceness,* and so on. The suffix *–tion* is commonly used to transform a verb into its noun form, as with *converse* and *conversation or move* and *motion.* Thus, if readers are unfamiliar with the second form of a word, knowing the meaning of the transforming suffix can help them determine meaning.

While knowing prefix meanings helps ESL and beginning readers learn new words, other readers take for granted the meanings of known words. However, prefix knowledge will also benefit them for determining meanings or definitions of unfamiliar words. For example, native English speakers and readers familiar with recipes know what *preheat* means. Knowing that *pre-* means in advance can also inform them that *presume* means to assume in advance, that *prejudice* means advance judgment, and that this understanding can be applied to many other words beginning with *pre-*. Knowing that the prefix *dis-* indicates opposition informs the meanings of words like *disbar, disagree, disestablish,* and many more. Knowing *dys-* means bad, impaired, abnormal, or difficult informs *dyslogistic, dysfunctional, dysphagia,* and *dysplasia.*

English Conventions
© Mometrix Media - flashcardsecrets.com/louisiana
English I

Describe synonyms and antonyms and discuss what is necessary to designate two words as synonymous.

English Conventions
© Mometrix Media - flashcardsecrets.com/louisiana
English I

Discuss the relationship between antonyms.

English Conventions
© Mometrix Media - flashcardsecrets.com/louisiana
English I

Define what affixes are in the English language. Differentially define derivational versus inflectional affixes and give examples of each. Name some common types and positions of English affixes.

English Conventions
© Mometrix Media - flashcardsecrets.com/louisiana
English I

Explain with the use of examples how knowing the origins of word roots, prefixes, and suffixes can help readers to determine the meanings of new or unfamiliar vocabulary words.

English Conventions
© Mometrix Media - flashcardsecrets.com/louisiana
English I

Explain using examples how knowledge of prefixes can help readers determine the meanings of unfamiliar words.

English Conventions
© Mometrix Media - flashcardsecrets.com/louisiana
English I

Using some examples, explain how a knowledge of suffixes can help readers to deduce the meanings of words they may not know.

A graph is a visual representation that exhibits a relationship, often functional, between two sets of numbers as a set of points having coordinates determined by the relationship. The term **chart** may be used as a synonym for graph, or it may refer to a specialized kind of map, such as a nautical chart. There are many different methods of displaying data in graphs and charts; most include the plotting of data in **two dimensions**. Many of these diagrams include several basic features. First of all, a title indicates the purpose and content of a graph or chart. Most diagrams have a **horizontal axis** (the x-axis) and a **vertical axis** (the y-axis); the intersection of these axes, where the value of each variable equals zero, is referred to as the **origin**. These axes are labeled to identify the variable being plotted and/or the range of values of that variable. Generally, independent variables (such as time) are represented on the x-axis, and dependent variables (such as temperature) are represented on the y-axis.

To evaluate the effectiveness of an appeal, it is important to consider the author's purpose for writing. Any appeals an author uses in their argument must be relevant to the argument's goal. For example, a writer that argues for the reclassification of Pluto, but primarily uses appeals to emotion, will not have an effective argument. This writer should focus on using appeals to logic and support their argument with provable facts. While most arguments should include appeals to logic, emotion, and credibility, some arguments only call for one or two of these types of appeal. Evidence can support an appeal, but the evidence must be relevant to truly strengthen the appeal's effectiveness. If the writer arguing for Pluto's reclassification uses the reasons for Jupiter's classification as evidence, their argument would be weak. This information may seem relevant because it is related to the classification of planets. However, this classification is highly dependent on the size of the celestial object, and Jupiter is significantly bigger than Pluto. This use of evidence is illogical and does not support the appeal. Even when appropriate evidence and appeals are used, appeals and arguments lose their effectiveness when they create logical fallacies.

A line graph is a type of chart that is useful in representing relationships between sets of data. **Line graphs** are often used to show changes in a variable over time. For instance, in a graph of sale trends for a major company, a time scale (such as years or months) is laid out along the x-axis and an amount scale is oriented along the y-axis. Then, the respective sales figures corresponding to each time unit are plotted on the graph; these data points are connected with a line whose curvature conveys general tendencies about changes in sales over time. This feature of line graphs enables viewers to make educated predictions about future trends as well. In economics, a line graph may be used to show the relationship between quantity (on the x-axis) and price (on the y-axis). By connecting plotted points with lines, economists can identify changes in price as they relate to changes in the available quantities of goods.

A pie chart, also referred to as a circle graph, is a method of data representation that does not use the axes common in other kinds of graphs, and therefore does not involve the plotting of data in two dimensions. **Pie charts** are based on percentages of a total quantity; a full circle represents one hundred percent. This type of chart is useful when this quantity is known and the chart's creator wishes to convey the relative sizes of the "pieces" which add up to that total. For example, if a geographer knows the total number of people worldwide who identify themselves as having religious beliefs, he or she might create a pie chart to show what percentage of that total describes themselves as Muslims, Christians, Jews, etc. Percentages are converted to numbers of degrees and represented as sections of the circle. A **100 percent bar chart** uses represents percentages as proportional sections of a bar.

A scatter plot is a type of display that shows the values for two variables for a set of data. Like bar and line graphs, **scatter plots** use x- and y-axes to plot data points. However, their specific purpose is to display how one variable affects another. This relationship is referred to as **correlation**. Correlation between variables is identified through the examination of a large quantity of data, represented on the graph as points. The closer the points come to forming a straight line, the stronger the relationship (and the higher the correlation) between the variables. If the line formed by the points extends from a high point on the y-axis to a high value on the x-axis, the correlation is negative. Conversely, if the line extends from the origin to high x- and y-values, the correlation between the two variables is positive. One might use a scatter plot to examine the relationship between education and income by aligning education level along the x-axis of a graph and yearly income along the y-axis, and then plotting data points for a group of individuals.

A bar graph is a type of chart that is useful in **comparing quantities**. This type of chart is similar to a line graph in that each involves the placement of variables along two axes. Instead of displaying values as points on the grid, however, a **bar chart** uses rectangular bars extending from an axis and leveling off at the appropriate points. In other words, the length of a bar representing a particular variable conveys the value of that variable. Bar graphs may be vertical (in which independent variables are oriented along the x-axis and the rectangles extend vertically) or horizontal (in which independent variables are laid out along the y-axis and the rectangles extend horizontally). This type of graph aids in the observation of differences among similar things. For example, a bar chart may display the variations in population among several major cities. In a pictograph, small icons or figures relating are used in lieu of rectangles to represent values. This type of graph is eye-catching and instantly conveys the purpose of the graph.

Reading
© Mometrix Media - flashcardsecrets.com/louisiana
English I

Discuss how an author's purpose affects the effectiveness of an appeal.

Reading
© Mometrix Media - flashcardsecrets.com/louisiana
English I

Describe graphs and charts.

Reading
© Mometrix Media - flashcardsecrets.com/louisiana
English I

Describe pie charts and 100 percent bar charts.

Reading
© Mometrix Media - flashcardsecrets.com/louisiana
English I

Describe line graphs.

Reading
© Mometrix Media - flashcardsecrets.com/louisiana
English I

Describe bar graphs.

Reading
© Mometrix Media - flashcardsecrets.com/louisiana
English I

Describe scatter plots.

The text used to support an argument can be the argument's downfall if the text is not credible. A text is **credible**, or believable, when its author is knowledgeable and objective, or unbiased. The author's motivations for writing the text play a critical role in determining the credibility of the text and must be evaluated when assessing that credibility. Reports written about the ozone layer by an environmental scientist and a hairdresser will have a different level of credibility.

The term **text evidence** refers to information that supports a main point or minor points and can help lead the reader to a conclusion about the text's credibility. Information used as text evidence is precise, descriptive, and factual. A main point is often followed by supporting details that provide evidence to back up a claim. For example, a passage may include the claim that winter occurs during opposite months in the Northern and Southern hemispheres. Text evidence for this claim may include examples of countries where winter occurs in opposite months. Stating that the tilt of the Earth as it rotates around the sun causes winter to occur at different times in separate hemispheres is another example of text evidence. Text evidence can come from common knowledge, but it is also valuable to include text evidence from credible, relevant outside sources.

Evidence that supports the thesis and additional arguments needs to be provided. Most arguments must be supported by facts or statistics. A fact is something that is known with certainty, has been verified by several independent individuals, and can be proven to be true. In addition to facts, examples and illustrations can support an argument by adding an emotional component. With this component, you persuade readers in ways that facts and statistics cannot. The emotional component is effective when used alongside objective information that can be confirmed.

When authors give both sides to the argument, they build trust with their readers. As a reader, you should start with an undecided or neutral position. If an author presents only his or her side to the argument, then they are not exhibiting credibility and are weakening their argument.

Building common ground with readers can be effective for persuading neutral, skeptical, or opposed readers. Sharing values with undecided readers can allow people to switch positions without giving up what they feel is important. People who may oppose a position need to feel that they can change their minds without betraying who they are as a person. This appeal to having an open mind can be a powerful tool in arguing a position without antagonizing other views. Objections can be countered on a point-by-point basis or in a summary paragraph. Be mindful of how an author points out flaws in counter arguments. If they are unfair to the other side of the argument, then you should lose trust with the author.

Sometimes, authors will appeal to the reader's emotion in an attempt to persuade or to distract the reader from the weakness of the argument. For instance, the author may try to inspire the pity of the reader by delivering a heart-rending story. An author also might use the bandwagon approach, in which he suggests that his opinion is correct because it is held by the majority. Some authors resort to name-calling, in which insults and harsh words are delivered to the opponent in an attempt to distract. In advertising, a common appeal is the celebrity testimonial, in which a famous person endorses a product. Of course, the fact that a famous person likes something should not really mean anything to the reader. These and other emotional appeals are usually evidence of poor reasoning and a weak argument.

The first three reader steps to **evaluate an author's argument** are to identify the **author's assumptions**, identify the **supporting evidence**, and decide **whether the evidence is relevant**. For example, if an author is not an expert on a particular topic, then that author's personal experience or opinion might not be relevant. The fourth step is to assess the **author's objectivity**. For example, consider whether the author introduces clear, understandable supporting evidence and facts to support the argument. The fifth step is evaluating whether the author's **argument is complete**. When authors give sufficient support for their arguments and also anticipate and respond effectively to opposing arguments or objections to their points, their arguments are complete. However, some authors omit information that could detract from their arguments. If instead they stated this information and refuted it, it would strengthen their arguments. The sixth step in evaluating an author's argumentative writing is to assess whether the **argument is valid**. Providing clear, logical reasoning makes an author's argument valid. Readers should ask themselves whether the author's points follow a sequence that makes sense, and whether each point leads to the next. The seventh step is to determine whether the author's **argument is credible**, meaning that it is convincing and believable. Arguments that are not valid are not credible, so step seven depends on step six. Readers should be mindful of their own biases as they evaluate and should not expect authors to conclusively prove their arguments, but rather to provide effective support and reason.

In argumentative writing, the argument is a belief, position, or opinion that the author wants to convince readers to believe as well. For the first step, readers should identify the **issue**. Some issues are controversial, meaning people disagree about them. Gun control, foreign policy, and the death penalty are all controversial issues. The next step is to determine the **author's position** on the issue. That position or viewpoint constitutes the author's argument. Readers should then identify the **author's assumptions**: things he or she accepts, believes, or takes for granted without needing proof. Inaccurate or illogical assumptions produce flawed arguments and can mislead readers. Readers should identify what kinds of **supporting evidence** the author offers, such as research results, personal observations or experiences, case studies, facts, examples, expert testimony and opinions, and comparisons. Readers should decide how relevant this support is to the argument.

Reading
© Mometrix Media - flashcardsecrets.com/louisiana
English I

Explain what is meant by the term text evidence and indicate how it can be used to draw a conclusion.

Reading
© Mometrix Media - flashcardsecrets.com/louisiana
English I

Explain how to evaluate the credibility of a text.

Reading
© Mometrix Media - flashcardsecrets.com/louisiana
English I

Describe how an author may appeal to the reader's emotion.

Reading
© Mometrix Media - flashcardsecrets.com/louisiana
English I

Discuss the use of counter arguments in an argumentative or persuasive essay.

Reading
© Mometrix Media - flashcardsecrets.com/louisiana
English I

Briefly define an author's argument in argumentative writing. Explain the first three of seven steps for evaluating an author's argument.

Reading
© Mometrix Media - flashcardsecrets.com/louisiana
English I

Summarize the first three steps for readers to evaluate an author's argument in argumentative or persuasive writing. Then detail the fourth, fifth, sixth, and seventh steps for evaluating author arguments.

Informational text can be **descriptive**, appealing to the five senses and answering the questions what, who, when, where, and why. Another method of structuring informational text is sequence and order. **Chronological** texts relate events in the sequence that they occurred, from start to finish, while how-to texts organize information into a series of instructions in the sequence in which the steps should be followed. **Comparison-contrast** structures of informational text describe various ideas to their readers by pointing out how things or ideas are similar and how they are different. **Cause and effect** structures of informational text describe events that occurred and identify the causes or reasons that those events occurred. **Problem and solution** structures of informational texts introduce and describe problems and offer one or more solutions for each problem described.

With informational text, reader comprehension depends not only on recalling important statements and details, but also on reader inferences based on examples and details. Readers add information from the text to what they already know to draw inferences about the text. These inferences help the readers to fill in the information that the text does not explicitly state, enabling them to understand the text better. When reading a nonfictional autobiography or biography, for example, the most appropriate inferences might concern the events in the book, the actions of the subject of the autobiography or biography, and the message the author means to convey. When reading a nonfictional expository (informational) text, the reader would best draw inferences about problems and their solutions, and causes and their effects. When reading a nonfictional persuasive text, the reader will want to infer ideas supporting the author's message and intent.

In some informational texts, readers find it easy to identify the author's point of view and purpose, such as when the author explicitly states his or her position and reason for writing. But other texts are more difficult, either because of the content or because the authors give neutral or balanced viewpoints. This is particularly true in scientific texts, in which authors may state the purpose of their research in the report, but never state their point of view except by interpreting evidence or data.

To analyze text and identify point of view or purpose, readers should ask themselves the following four questions:

1. With what main point or idea does this author want to persuade readers to agree?
2. How does this author's word choice affect the way that readers consider this subject?
3. How do this author's choices of examples and facts affect the way that readers consider this subject?
4. What is it that this author wants to accomplish by writing this text?

Informational authors' purposes are why they write texts. Readers must determine authors' motivations and goals. Readers gain greater insight into a text by considering the author's motivation. This develops critical reading skills. Readers perceive writing as a person's voice, not simply printed words. Uncovering author motivations and purposes empowers readers to know what to expect from the text, read for relevant details, evaluate authors and their work critically, and respond effectively to the motivations and persuasions of the text. The main idea of a text is what the reader is supposed to understand from reading it; the purpose of the text is why the author has written it and what the author wants readers to do with its information. Authors state some purposes clearly, while other purposes may be unstated but equally significant. When stated purposes contradict other parts of a text, the author may have a hidden agenda. Readers can better evaluate a text's effectiveness, whether they agree or disagree with it, and why they agree or disagree through identifying unstated author purposes.

There are many ways authors can support their claims, arguments, beliefs, ideas, and reasons for writing in informational texts. For example, authors can appeal to readers' sense of **logic** by communicating their reasoning through a carefully sequenced series of logical steps to help "prove" the points made. Authors can appeal to readers' **emotions** by using descriptions and words that evoke feelings of sympathy, sadness, anger, righteous indignation, hope, happiness, or any other emotion to reinforce what they express and share with their audience. Authors may appeal to the **moral** or **ethical values** of readers by using words and descriptions that can convince readers that something is right or wrong. By relating personal anecdotes, authors can supply readers with more accessible, realistic examples of points they make, as well as appealing to their emotions. They can provide supporting evidence by reporting case studies. They can also illustrate their points by making analogies to which readers can better relate.

When evaluating an informational text, the first step is to identify the argument's conclusion. Then identify the author's premises that support the conclusion. Try to paraphrase premises for clarification and make the conclusion and premises fit. List all premises first, sequentially numbered, then finish with the conclusion. Identify any premises or assumptions not stated by the author but required for the stated premises to support the conclusion. Read word assumptions sympathetically, as the author might. Evaluate whether premises reasonably support the conclusion. For inductive reasoning, the reader should ask if the premises are true, if they support the conclusion, and if so, how strongly. For deductive reasoning, the reader should ask if the argument is valid or invalid. If all premises are true, then the argument is valid unless the conclusion can be false. If it can, then the argument is invalid. An invalid argument can be made valid through alterations such as the addition of needed premises.

Reading
© Mometrix Media - flashcardsecrets.com/louisiana
English I

Describe generally the process for making inferences about informational text when reading it, including what kinds of reader inferences are most suited to different types of informational texts.

Reading
© Mometrix Media - flashcardsecrets.com/louisiana
English I

Identify and define five different structures or organizational patterns found in informational texts.

Reading
© Mometrix Media - flashcardsecrets.com/louisiana
English I

Discuss the process of determining an informational author's purpose for writing, including the difference between main ideas and purposes, and stated purposes versus unstated ones.

Reading
© Mometrix Media - flashcardsecrets.com/louisiana
English I

Relate several ways to identify an author's point of view or purpose in an informational text.

Reading
© Mometrix Media - flashcardsecrets.com/louisiana
English I

Describe some steps that readers can take for evaluating the arguments made by writers of informational text.

Reading
© Mometrix Media - flashcardsecrets.com/louisiana
English I

Discuss some ways that authors use rhetoric to support their main points, ideas, viewpoints, and/or purpose in informational texts.

When informational text states something explicitly, the reader is told by the author exactly what is meant, which can include the author's interpretation or perspective of events. For example, a professor writes, "I have seen students go into an absolute panic just because they weren't able to complete the exam in the time they were allotted." This explicitly tells the reader that the students were afraid, and by using the words "just because," the writer indicates their fear was exaggerated out of proportion relative to what happened. However, another professor writes, "I have had students come to me, their faces drained of all color, saying 'We weren't able to finish the exam.'" This is an example of implicit meaning: the second writer did not state explicitly that the students were panicked. Instead, he wrote a description of their faces being "drained of all color." From this description, the reader can infer that the students were so frightened that their faces paled.

As in fictional literature, informational text also uses both **literal language**, which means just what it says, and **figurative language**, which imparts more than literal meaning. For example, an informational text author might use a simile or direct comparison, such as writing that a racehorse "ran like the wind." Informational text authors also use metaphors or implied comparisons, such as "the cloud of the Great Depression." Imagery may also appear in informational texts to increase the reader's understanding of ideas and concepts discussed in the text.

Writing about **technical subjects** for **non-technical readers** differs from writing for colleagues because authors place more importance on delivering a critical message than on imparting the maximum technical content possible. Technical authors also must assume that non-technical audiences do not have the expertise to comprehend extremely scientific or technical messages, concepts, and terminology. They must resist the temptation to impress audiences with their scientific knowledge and expertise and remember that their primary purpose is to communicate a message that non-technical readers will understand, feel, and respond to. Non-technical and technical styles include similarities. Both should formally cite any references or other authors' work utilized in the text. Both must follow intellectual property and copyright regulations. This includes the author's protecting his or her own rights, or a public domain statement, as he or she chooses.

Technical language is more impersonal than literary and vernacular language. Passive voice makes the tone impersonal. For example, instead of writing, "We found this a central component of protein metabolism," scientists write, "This was found a central component of protein metabolism." While science professors have traditionally instructed students to avoid active voice because it leads to first-person ("I" and "we") usage, science editors today find passive voice dull and weak. Many journal articles combine both. Tone in technical science writing should be detached, concise, and professional. While one may normally write, "This chemical has to be available for proteins to be digested," professionals write technically, "The presence of this chemical is required for the enzyme to break the covalent bonds of proteins." The use of technical language appeals to both technical and non-technical audiences by displaying the author or speaker's understanding of the subject and suggesting their credibility regarding the message they are communicating.

Authors of technical information sometimes must write using non-technical language that readers outside their disciplinary fields can comprehend. They should use not only non-technical terms, but also normal, everyday language to accommodate readers whose native language is different than the language the text is written in. For example, instead of writing that "eustatic changes like thermal expansion are causing hazardous conditions in the littoral zone," an author would do better to write that "a rising sea level is threatening the coast." When technical terms cannot be avoided, authors should also define or explain them using non-technical language. Although authors must cite references and acknowledge their use of others' work, they should avoid the kinds of references or citations that they would use in scientific journals—unless they reinforce author messages. They should not use endnotes, footnotes, or any other complicated referential techniques because non-technical journal publishers usually do not accept them. Including high-resolution illustrations, photos, maps, or satellite images and incorporating multimedia into digital publications will enhance non-technical writing about technical subjects. Technical authors may publish using non-technical language in e-journals, trade journals, specialty newsletters, and daily newspapers.

Writers of technical or scientific material may need to write for many non-technical audiences. Some readers have no technical or scientific background, and those who do may not be in the same field as the authors. Government and corporate policymakers and budget managers need technical information they can understand for decision-making. Citizens affected by technology or science are a different audience. Non-governmental organizations can encompass many of the preceding groups. Elementary and secondary school programs also need non-technical language for presenting technical subject matter. Additionally, technical authors will need to use non-technical language when collecting consumer responses to surveys, presenting scientific or para-scientific material to the public, writing about the history of science, and writing about science and technology in developing countries.

Reading
© Mometrix Media - flashcardsecrets.com/louisiana
English I

Define and give an example of figurative versus literal language in informational text. Briefly discuss the use of imagery in informational texts.

Reading
© Mometrix Media - flashcardsecrets.com/louisiana
English I

Give an example of the difference between how informational text states something explicitly and how implicit meaning can be inferred from text that does not state it directly.

Reading
© Mometrix Media - flashcardsecrets.com/louisiana
English I

Discuss some characteristics of technical language in informational text, including voice, tone, mood, and how it differs from literary and vernacular (everyday) language.

Reading
© Mometrix Media - flashcardsecrets.com/louisiana
English I

Explain some differences and similarities between writing about technical subjects for non-technical readers and writing for about technical subjects for technical colleagues in their field.

Reading
© Mometrix Media - flashcardsecrets.com/louisiana
English I

Give some examples of audiences for whom writers of technical material need to use non-technical language. Explain why such authors need to use a different style of writing.

Reading
© Mometrix Media - flashcardsecrets.com/louisiana
English I

Relate a few tips for authors of technical information to write for non-technical readers, including some things to avoid, and where authors may publish such writing.

Despite virtually limitless interpretations, one way to view Hamlet's tragic error generally is as indecision. He suffers the classic revenge tragedy's conflict of whether to suffer with his knowledge of his mother's and uncle's assassination of his father, or to exact his own revenge and justice against Claudius, who has assumed the throne after his crime went unknown and unpunished. Hamlet's famous soliloquy, "To be or not to be" reflects this dilemma. Hamlet muses "Whether 'tis nobler in the mind to suffer the slings and arrows of outrageous fortune, / Or to take arms against a sea of troubles, / And by opposing end them?" Hamlet both longs for and fears death, as "the dread of something after death … makes us rather bear those ills we have / Than fly to others that we know not … Thus, conscience does make cowards of us all." For most of the play, Hamlet struggles with his responsibility to avenge his father, who was killed by Hamlet's uncle, Claudius. So, Hamlet's tragic error at first might be considered a lack of action. But he then makes several attempts at revenge, each of which end in worse tragedy, until his efforts are ended by the final tragedy—Hamlet's own death.

Along with Aristotelian definitions of comedy and tragedy, ancient Greece was the origin of the **revenge tragedy**. This genre became highly popular in Renaissance England, and is still popular today in contemporary movies. In a revenge tragedy, the protagonist has suffered a serious wrong, such as the murder of a family member. However, the wrongdoer has not been punished. In contemporary plots, this often occurs when some legal technicality has interfered with the miscreant's conviction and sentencing, or when authorities are unable to locate and apprehend the criminal. The protagonist then faces the conflict of suffering this injustice, or exacting his or her own justice by seeking revenge. Greek revenge tragedies include *Agamemnon* and *Medea*. Playwright Thomas Kyd's *The Spanish Tragedy* (1582-1592) is credited with beginning the Elizabethan genre of revenge tragedies. Shakespearean revenge tragedies include *Hamlet* (1599-1602) and *Titus Andronicus* (1588-1593). A Jacobean example is Thomas Middleton's *The Revenger's Tragedy* (1606, 1607).

Emails and letters communicate in writing for personal and for business purposes. In both letters and emails the format and style will depend on the relationship between the sender and the recipient. Family members and friends will use a very informal, colloquial language with each other. Emails or letters sent to a company asking for a job will be formal and structured. Read your assignment carefully, and determine how the sender and recipient are related. Use the degree of formality that matches that connection. Whether formal or informal, organize your thoughts and present them in a clear, logical manner. Start with an appropriate salutation and end with a signature.

A memo (short for memorandum) is usually a short, concise written piece used at work to inform, instruct, or remind about a particular subject. Memos do not have to be very formal, but they do not tend to be too informal either. They must be very clear. The heading of a memo should start with the date, the recipient, and the sender. Include a Subject line at the beginning stating, in a few words, the topic of the memo (see example of heading below). Use short paragraphs and simple sentences. Include lists and use specific vocabulary. Avoid the passive voice and unnecessary details. Memos do not include a salutation and signature at the bottom.

MEMORANDUM
July 13, 2012
To: Paul Johnson
From: Lisa Smith
SUBJECT: Personnel changes

Illustrations and **photographs** are pictures that visually emphasize important points in text. The captions below the illustrations explain what those images show. Charts and tables are visual forms of information that make something easier to understand quickly. Diagrams are drawings that show relationships or explain a process. Graphs visually show the relationships among multiple sets of information plotted along vertical and horizontal axes. Maps show geographical information visually to help readers understand the relative locations of places covered in the text. Timelines are visual graphics that show historical events in chronological order to help readers see their sequence.

The **title of a text** gives readers some idea of its content. The **table of contents** is a list near the beginning of a text, showing the book's sections and chapters and their coinciding page numbers. This gives readers an overview of the whole text and helps them find specific chapters easily. An **appendix**, at the back of the book or document, includes important information that is not present in the main text. Also at the back, an **index** lists the book's important topics alphabetically with their page numbers to help readers find them easily. **Glossaries**, usually found at the backs of books, list technical terms alphabetically with their definitions to aid vocabulary learning and comprehension. Boldface print is used to emphasize certain words, often identifying words included in the text's glossary where readers can look up their definitions. **Headings** separate sections of text and show the topic of each. **Subheadings** divide subject headings into smaller, more specific categories to help readers organize information. **Footnotes**, at the bottom of the page, give readers more information, such as citations or links. **Bullet points** list items separately, making facts and ideas easier to see and understand. A **sidebar** is a box of information to one side of the main text giving additional information, often on a more focused or in-depth example of a topic.

Briefly summarize the origin and progress of the revenge tragedy as one form of tragic drama. Include examples.

Discuss one possible interpretation of what the tragic hero Hamlet's "tragic flaw" or tragic error may have been in William Shakespeare's tragedy *Hamlet*.

Describe the process for writing a memo.

Describe the process of writing emails and letters for personal and business purposes.

Identify 10 text features in informational texts and briefly state how they contribute to the text's central ideas.

List some visual components that are often included in texts and how they can help readers better comprehend the text.

Romantic comedies are probably the most popular of the types of comedy, in both live theater performances and movies. They include not only humor and a happy ending, but also love. In the typical plot of a **romantic comedy**, two people well suited to one another are either brought together for the first time, or reconciled after being separated. They are usually both sympathetic characters and seem destined to be together, yet they are separated by some intervening complication, such as ex-lovers, interfering parents or friends, or differences in social class. The happy ending is achieved through the lovers overcoming all these obstacles. William Shakespeare's *Much Ado About Nothing*, Walt Disney's version of *Cinderella* (1950), and Broadway musical *Guys and Dolls* (1955) are example of romantic comedies. Many live-action movies are also examples of romantic comedies, such as *The Princess Bride* (1987), *Sleepless in Seattle* (1993), *You've Got Mail* (1998), and *Forget Paris* (1995).

The **farce** is a zany, goofy type of comedy that includes pratfalls and other forms of slapstick humor. The characters in a farce tend to be ridiculous or fantastical in nature. The plot also tends to contain highly improbable events, featuring complications and twists that continue throughout, and incredible coincidences that would likely never occur in reality. Mistaken identity, deceptions, and disguises are common devices used in farcical comedies. Shakespeare's play *The Comedy of Errors,* with its cases of accidental mistaken identity and slapstick, is an example of farce. Contemporary examples of farce include the Marx Brothers' movies, the Three Stooges movies and TV episodes, and the *Pink Panther* movie series.

The opposite of comedy is tragedy, portraying a hero's fall in fortune. While by classical definitions, tragedies could be sad, Aristotle went further, requiring that they depict suffering and pain to cause "terror and pity" in audiences. Additionally, he decreed that tragic heroes be basically good, admirable, or noble, and that their downfalls result from personal action, choice, or error, not by bad luck or accident.

Satires generally mock and lampoon human foolishness and vices. **Satirical comedies** fit the classical definition of comedy by depicting a main character's rise in fortune, but they also fit the definition of satire by making that main character either a fool, morally corrupt, or cynical in attitude. All or most of the other characters in the satirical comedy display similar foibles. These include gullible types, such as cuckolded spouses and dupes, and deceptive types, such as tricksters, con artists, criminals, hypocrites, and fortune seekers, who prey on the gullible. Some classical examples of satirical comedies include *The Birds* by ancient Greek comedic playwright Aristophanes, and *Volpone* by 17th-century poet and playwright Ben Jonson, who made the comedy of humors popular. When satirical comedy is extended to extremes, it becomes **black comedy**, wherein the comedic occurrences are grotesque or terrible.

Georg Wilhelm Friedrich Hegel (1770-1831) proposed a different theory of tragedy than Aristotle (384-322 BC), which was also very influential. Whereas Aristotle's criteria involved character and plot, Hegel defined tragedy as a dynamic conflict of opposite forces or rights. For example, if an individual believes in the moral philosophy of the conscientious objector (i.e., that fighting in wars is morally wrong) but is confronted with being drafted into military service, this conflict would fit Hegel's definition of a tragic plot premise. Hegel theorized that a tragedy must involve some circumstance in which two values, or two rights, are fatally at odds with one another and conflict directly. Hegel did not view this as good triumphing over evil, or evil winning out over good, but rather as one good fighting against another good unto death. He saw this conflict of two goods as truly tragic. In ancient Greek playwright Sophocles' tragedy *Antigone*, the main character experiences this tragic conflict between her public duties and her family and religious responsibilities.

In his *Poetics,* Aristotle identified various elements that appear in Greek tragedies:

Anagnorisis: Meaning tragic insight or recognition, this is a moment of realization by a tragic hero or heroine that he or she has become enmeshed in a "web of fate."

Catharsis: Meaning an emotional release on the part of the audience.

Hamartia: This is often called a "tragic flaw," but is better described as a tragic error. *Hamartia* is an archery term meaning a shot missing the bull's eye, used here as a metaphor for a mistake—often a simple one—which results in catastrophe.

Hubris: While often called "pride," this is actually translated as "violent transgression," and signifies an arrogant overstepping of moral or cultural bounds—the sin of the tragic hero who over-presumes or over-aspires.

Mimesis: This refers to the idea that works of art reflect the real world, including individuals, nature, human behavior, and social order.

Nemesis: translated as "retribution," this represents the cosmic punishment or payback that the tragic hero ultimately receives for committing hubristic acts.

Peripateia: Literally "turning," this is a plot reversal consisting of a tragic hero's pivotal action, which changes his or her status from safe to endangered.

Spectacle: Visual elements of the story, in the context of dramatic plays.

Reading
© Mometrix Media - flashcardsecrets.com/louisiana
English I

Describe some characteristics of farce as one type of dramatic comedy, giving a few examples.

Reading
© Mometrix Media - flashcardsecrets.com/louisiana
English I

Identify several of the characteristics and examples of romantic comedy as one form of dramatic comedy.

Reading
© Mometrix Media - flashcardsecrets.com/louisiana
English I

Describe some of the characteristics of satirical comedy and black comedy as forms of comedic drama and give some examples.

Reading
© Mometrix Media - flashcardsecrets.com/louisiana
English I

Discuss how the Classical definition tragedy differs from the contemporary one.

Reading
© Mometrix Media - flashcardsecrets.com/louisiana
English I

Aristotle identified various elements that appear in Greek tragedies. Define the terms, including: anagnorisis, catharsis, hamartia, hubris, mimesis, nemesis, peripateia, and spectacle.

Reading
© Mometrix Media - flashcardsecrets.com/louisiana
English I

Discuss the theory of tragedy proposed by Hegel, including differences between Hegelian and Aristotelian tragedy. Identify some of Hegel's criteria, naming an ancient Greek drama that exemplified these.

English **drama** originally developed from religious ritual. Early Christians established traditions of presenting pageants or mystery plays, traveling on wagons and carts through the streets to depict Biblical events. Medieval tradition assigned responsibility for performing specific plays to the different guilds. In Middle English, "mystery" referred to craft, or trade, and religious ritual and truth. Historically, mystery plays were to be reproduced exactly the same every time they were performed, like religious rituals. However, some performers introduced individual interpretations of roles and even improvised. Thus, drama was born. Narrative detail and nuanced acting were evident in mystery cycles by the Middle Ages. As individualized performance evolved, plays on other subjects also developed. Middle English mystery plays that still exist include the York Cycle, Coventry Cycle, Chester Mystery Plays, N-Town Plays, and Towneley/Wakefield Plays. In recent times, these plays began to draw interest again, and several modern actors, such as Dame Judi Dench, began their careers with mystery plays.

Today, most people equate the idea of **comedy** with something funny, and of **tragedy** with something sad. However, the ancient Greeks defined these differently. Comedy needed not be humorous or amusing; it needed only a happy ending. The classical definition of comedy, as included in Aristotle's works, is any work that tells the story of a sympathetic main character's rise in fortune. According to Aristotle, protagonists need not be heroic or exemplary, nor evil or worthless, but ordinary people of unremarkable morality. Comic figures who were sympathetic were usually of humble origins, proving their "natural nobility" through their actions as they were tested. Characters born into nobility were often satirized as self-important or pompous.

When Shakespeare was writing, during the Elizabethan period of the Renaissance, Aristotle's version of comedies was popular. While some of Shakespeare's comedies were humorous and others were not, all had happy endings. *A Comedy of Errors* is a farce. Based and expanding on a Classical Roman comedy, it is lighthearted and includes slapstick humor and mistaken identity. *Much Ado About Nothing* is a romantic comedy. It incorporates some more serious themes, including social mores, perceived infidelity, marriage's duality as both trap and ideal, honor and its loss, public shame, and deception, but also much witty dialogue and a happy ending.

Sylvia Plath's villanelle "Mad Girl's Love Song" narrows the scope from universal to personal but keeps the theme of cycle. The two repeated lines, "I shut my eyes and all the world drops dead" and "(I think I made you up inside my head.)" reflect the existential viewpoint that nothing exists in any absolute reality outside of our own perceptions. In the first stanza, the middle line, "I lift my lids and all is born again," in its recreating the world, bridges between the repeated refrain statements—one of obliterating reality, the other of having constructed her lover's existence. Unlike other villanelles wherein key lines are subtly altered in their repetitions, Plath repeats these exactly each time. This reflects the young woman's love, constant throughout the poem as it neither fades nor progresses.

In the Middle Ages, plays were commonly composed in **verse**. By the time of the Renaissance, Shakespeare and other dramatists wrote plays that mixed **prose**, **rhymed verse**, and **blank verse**. The traditions of costumes and masks were seen in ancient Greek drama, medieval mystery plays, and Renaissance drama. Conventions like **asides**, in which actors make comments directly to the audience unheard by other characters, and **soliloquies** were also common during Shakespeare's Elizabethan dramatic period. **Monologues** date back to ancient Greek drama. Elizabethan dialogue tended to use colloquial prose for lower-class characters' speech and stylized verse for upper-class characters. Another Elizabethan convention was the play-within-a-play, as in *Hamlet*. As drama moved toward realism, dialogue became less poetic and more conversational, as in most modern English-language plays. Contemporary drama, both onstage and onscreen, includes a convention of **breaking the fourth wall**, as actors directly face and address audiences.

William Shakespeare lived in England from 1564-1616. He was a poet and playwright of the Renaissance period in Western culture. He is generally considered the foremost dramatist in world literature and the greatest author to write in the English language. He wrote many poems, particularly sonnets, of which 154 survive today, and approximately 38 plays. Though his sonnets are greater in number and are very famous, he is best known for his plays, including comedies, tragedies, tragicomedies and historical plays. His play titles include: *All's Well That Ends Well, As You Like It, The Comedy of Errors, Love's Labour's Lost, Measure for Measure, The Merchant of Venice, The Merry Wives of Windsor, A Midsummer Night's Dream, Much Ado About Nothing, The Taming of the Shrew, The Tempest, Twelfth Night, The Two Gentlemen of Verona, The Winter's Tale, King John, Richard II, Henry IV, Henry V, Richard III, Romeo and Juliet, Coriolanus, Titus Andronicus, Julius Caesar, Macbeth, Hamlet, Troilus and Cressida, King Lear, Othello, Antony and Cleopatra,* and *Cymbeline.* Some scholars have suggested that Christopher Marlowe wrote several of Shakespeare's works. While most scholars reject this theory, Shakespeare did pay homage to Marlowe, alluding to several of his characters, themes, or verbiage, as well as borrowing themes from several of his plays (e.g., Marlowe's *Jew of Malta* influenced Shakespeare's *Merchant of Venice*).

Reading
© Mometrix Media - flashcardsecrets.com/louisiana
English I

Discuss how Sylvia Plath uses the villanelle form to convey meaning in "Mad Girl's Love Song."

Reading
© Mometrix Media - flashcardsecrets.com/louisiana
English I

Explain how the genre of English drama originally developed within its historical and cultural context.

Reading
© Mometrix Media - flashcardsecrets.com/louisiana
English I

Describe some defining characteristics of the literary genre of drama, including how it has evolved through Medieval, Renaissance, modern, and contemporary forms.

Reading
© Mometrix Media - flashcardsecrets.com/louisiana
English I

Discuss how the Classical definition of comedy differs from the contemporary one.

Reading
© Mometrix Media - flashcardsecrets.com/louisiana
English I

Identify the role of William Shakespeare in world and English literature, including where and when he lived, what kinds of works he wrote, and titles of his major works.

Reading
© Mometrix Media - flashcardsecrets.com/louisiana
English I

Explain how Shakespearean comedy was influenced by Classical Greek philosophy of drama, including two examples.

When a poet uses a couplet—a stanza of two lines, rhymed or unrhymed—it can function as the answer to a question asked earlier in the poem, or the solution to a problem or riddle. Couplets can also enhance the establishment of a poem's mood, or clarify the development of a poem's theme. Another device to enhance thematic development is irony, which also communicates the poet's tone and draws the reader's attention to a point the poet is making. The use of meter gives a poem a rhythmic context, contributes to the poem's flow, makes it more appealing to the reader, can represent natural speech rhythms, and produces specific effects. For example, in "The Song of Hiawatha," Henry Wadsworth Longfellow uses trochaic (/ ᴜ) tetrameter (four beats per line) to evoke for readers the rhythms of Native American chanting: "*By* the *shores* of *Gitche Gumee*, / *By* the *shining Big*-Sea-*Water* / *Stood* the *wig*wam *of* Nokomis." (Italicized syllables are stressed; non-italicized syllables are unstressed.)

In enjambment, one sentence or clause in a poem does not end at the end of its line or verse, but runs over into the next line or verse. Clause endings coinciding with line endings give readers a feeling of completion, but enjambment influences readers to hurry to the next line to finish and understand the sentence. In his blank-verse epic religious poem "Paradise Lost," John Milton wrote: "Anon out of the earth a fabric huge / Rose like an exhalation, with the sound / Of dulcet symphonies and voices sweet, / Built like a temple, where pilasters round / Were set, and Doric pillars overlaid / With golden architrave." Only the third line is end-stopped. Milton, describing the palace of Pandemonium bursting from Hell up through the ground, reinforced this idea through phrases and clauses bursting through the boundaries of the lines. A **caesura** is a pause in mid-verse. Milton's commas in the third and fourth lines signal caesuras. They interrupt flow, making the narration jerky to imply that Satan's glorious-seeming palace has a shaky and unsound foundation.

Robert Frost's poem "Stopping by Woods on a Snowy Evening" (1923) is deceptively short and simple, with only four stanzas, each of only four lines, and short and simple words. Reinforcing this is Frost's use of regular rhyme and meter. The rhythm is iambic tetrameter throughout; the rhyme scheme is AABA in the first three stanzas and AAAA in the fourth. In an additional internal subtlety, B ending "here" in the first stanza is rhymed with A endings "queer," "near," and "year" of the second; B ending "lake" in the second is rhymed in A endings "shake," "mistake," and "flake" of the third. The final stanza's AAAA endings reinforce the ultimate darker theme. Though the first three stanzas seem to describe quietly watching snow fill the woods, the last stanza evokes the seductive pull of mysterious death: "The woods are lovely, dark and deep," countered by the obligations of living life: "But I have promises to keep, / And miles to go before I sleep, / And miles to go before I sleep." The last line's repetition strengthens Frost's message that despite death's temptation, life's course must precede it.

Wallace Stevens' short yet profound poem "The Snow Man" is reductionist: the snow man is a figure without human biases or emotions. Stevens begins, "One must have a mind of winter," the criterion for realizing nature and life does not inherently possess subjective qualities; we only invest it with these. Things are not as we see them; they simply are. The entire poem is one long sentence of clauses connected by conjunctions and commas, and modified by relative clauses and phrases. The successive phrases lead readers continually to reconsider as they read. Stevens' construction of the poem mirrors the meaning he conveys. With a mind of winter, the snow man, Stevens concludes, "nothing himself, beholds nothing that is not there, and the nothing that is."

A **villanelle** is a nineteen-line poem composed of five tercets and one quatrain. The defining characteristic is the repetition: two lines appear repeatedly throughout the poem. In Theodore Roethke's "The Waking," the two repeated lines are "I wake to sleep, and take my waking slow," and "I learn by going where I have to go." At first these sound paradoxical, but the meaning is gradually revealed through the poem. The repetition also fits with the theme of cycle: the paradoxes of waking to sleep, learning by going, and thinking by feeling represent a constant cycle through life. They also symbolize abandoning conscious rationalism to embrace spiritual vision. We wake from the vision to "Great Nature," and "take the lively air." "This shaking keeps me steady"—another paradox—juxtaposes and balances fear of mortality with ecstasy in embracing experience. The transcendent vision of all life's interrelationship demonstrates, "What falls away is always. And is near." Readers experience the poem holistically, like music, through Roethke's integration of theme, motion, and sound.

Through exaggeration, **hyperbole** communicates the strength of a poet's or persona's feelings and enhances the mood of the poem. **Imagery** appeals to the reader's senses, creating vivid mental pictures, evoking reader emotions and responses, and helping to develop themes. **Irony** also aids thematic development by drawing the reader's attention to the poet's point and communicating the poem's tone. Thematic development is additionally supported by the comparisons of **metaphors** and **similes**, which emphasize similarities, enhance imagery, and affect readers' perceptions. The use of **mood** communicates the atmosphere of a poem, builds a sense of tension, and evokes the reader's emotions. **Onomatopoeia** appeals to the reader's auditory sense and enhances sound imagery even when the poem is visual (read silently) rather than auditory (read aloud). **Rhyme** connects and unites verses, gives the rhyming words emphasis, and makes poems more fluent. **Symbolism** communicates themes, develops imagery, evokes readers' emotions, and elicits a response from the reader.

Reading
© Mometrix Media - flashcardsecrets.com/louisiana
English I

Give an example and explain how a poet uses structure to enhance meaning in a poem, specifically through the devices of enjambment and the caesura.

Reading
© Mometrix Media - flashcardsecrets.com/louisiana
English I

Explain how the effects of the poetic devices of couplets and meter enhance meaning in a poem.

Reading
© Mometrix Media - flashcardsecrets.com/louisiana
English I

Explicate how poet Wallace Stevens reflects content through structure in "The Snow Man" (1921).

Reading
© Mometrix Media - flashcardsecrets.com/louisiana
English I

Explicate how Robert Frost's use of simple language and regular structure contrast with and emphasize a profound underlying theme in "Stopping by Woods on a Snowy Evening" (1923).

Reading
© Mometrix Media - flashcardsecrets.com/louisiana
English I

Describe how the figurative devices of hyperbole, imagery, irony, metaphors, similes, mood, onomatopoeia, rhyme, and symbolism can contribute to meaning in poems and affect readers.

Visit *mometrix.com/academy* for a related video.
Enter video code: 177314

Reading
© Mometrix Media - flashcardsecrets.com/louisiana
English I

Explain some aspects of how the villanelle form, the harmony of content and structure, and of meaning and sound combine to total effect in Theodore Roethke's "The Waking."

The way a poem is structured can affect its meaning. Different structural choices can change the way a reader understands a poem, so poets are careful to ensure that the form they use reflects the message they want to convey. The main structural elements in poetry include **lines** and **stanzas**. The number of lines within a stanza and the number of stanzas vary between different poems, but some poetic forms require a poem to have a certain number of lines and stanzas. Some of these forms also require each line to conform to a certain meter, or number and pattern of syllables. Many forms are associated with a certain topic or tone because of their meter. Poetic forms include sonnets, concrete poems, haiku, and villanelles. Another popular form of poetry is free verse, which is poetry that does not conform to a particular meter or rhyme scheme.

The arrangement of lines and stanzas determines the speed at which a poem is read. Long lines are generally read more quickly since the reader is often eager to reach the end of the line and does not have to stop to find the next word. Short lines cause the reader to briefly pause and look to the next line, so their reading is slowed. These effects often contribute to the meaning a reader gleans from a poem, so poets aim to make the line length compatible with the tone of their message.

A less common form of poetry is concrete poetry, also called shape poetry. **Concrete poems** are arranged so the full poem takes a shape that is relevant to the poem's message. For example, a concrete poem about the beach may be arranged to look like a palm tree. This contributes to a poem's meaning by influencing which aspect of the poem or message that the reader focuses on. In the beach poem example, the image of the palm tree leads the reader to focus on the poem's setting and visual imagery. The reader may also look for or anticipate the mention of a palm tree in the poem. This technique allows the poet to direct the reader's attention and emphasize a certain element of their work.

The opening stanza of Romantic English poet, artist and printmaker William Blake's famous poem "The Tyger" demonstrates how a poet can create tension by using line length and punctuation independently of one another: "Tyger! Tyger! burning bright / In the forests of the night, / What immortal hand or eye / Could frame thy fearful symmetry?" The first three lines of this stanza are **trochaic** ($/\cup$), with "masculine" endings—that is, strongly stressed syllables at the ends of each of the lines. But Blake's punctuation contradicts this rhythmic regularity by not providing any divisions between the words "bright" and "In" or between "eye" and "Could." This irregular punctuation foreshadows how Blake disrupts the meter at the end of this first stanza by using a contrasting **dactyl** ($/\cup\cup$), with a "feminine" (unstressed) ending syllable in the last word, "symmetry." Thus Blake uses structural contrasts to heighten the intrigue of his work.

"To His Coy Mistress" begins, "Had we but world enough, and time, / This coyness, lady, were no crime." Using imagery, Andrew Marvell describes leisure they could enjoy if time were unlimited. Arguing for seduction, he continues famously, "But at my back I always hear/Time's winged chariot hurrying near; / And yonder all before us lie / Deserts of vast eternity." He depicts time as turning beauty to death and decay. Contradictory images in "amorous birds of prey" and "tear our pleasures with rough strife / Through the iron gates of life" overshadow romance with impending death, linking present pleasure with mortality and spiritual values with moral considerations. Marvell's concluding couplet summarizes *carpe diem*: "Thus, though we cannot make our sun / Stand still, yet we will make him run." "To the Virgins, to Make Much of Time" begins with the famous "Gather ye rosebuds while ye may." Rather than seduction to live for the present, Robert Herrick's experienced persona advises young women's future planning: "Old time is still a-flying / And this same flower that smiles today, / Tomorrow will be dying."

For example, Edgar Allan Poe's poem "The Raven" is written with mostly long lines. The poem's speaker experiences troubling events and becomes paranoid throughout the poem, and he narrates his racing thoughts. Poe's use of long lines leads the reader to read each line quickly, allowing their reading experience to resemble the thoughts of the narrator:

> Deep into that darkness peering, long I stood there wondering, fearing,
> Doubting, dreaming dreams no mortal ever dared to dream before;
> But the silence was unbroken, and the stillness gave no token,
> And the only word there spoken was the whispered word, "Lenore?"
> This I whispered, and an echo murmured back the word, "Lenore!"—
> Merely this and nothing more.

The poem's meter also contributes to its tone, but consider the same stanza written using shorter lines:

> Deep into that darkness peering,
> long I stood there wondering, fearing,
> Doubting, dreaming dreams no mortal
> ever dared to dream before;
> But the silence was unbroken,
> and the stillness gave no token,
> And the only word there spoken
> was the whispered word, "Lenore?"
> This I whispered, and an echo
> murmured back the word, "Lenore!"—
> Merely this and nothing more.

Breaking the lines apart creates longer pauses and a slower, more suspenseful experience for the reader. While the tone of the poem is dark and suspense is appropriate, the longer lines allow Poe to emphasize and show the narrator's emotions. The narrator's emotions are more important to the poem's meaning than the creation of suspense, making longer lines more suitable in this case.

Free verse is a very common form of poetry. Because **free verse** poetry does not always incorporate meter or rhyme, it relies more heavily on punctuation and structure to influence the reader's experience and create emphasis. Free verse poetry makes strategic use of the length and number of both lines and stanzas. While meter and rhyme direct the flow and tone of other types of poems, poets of free verse pieces use the characteristics of lines and stanzas to establish flow and tone, instead.

Free verse also uses punctuation in each line to create flow and tone. The punctuation in each line directs the reader to pause after certain words, allowing the poet to emphasize specific ideas or images to clearly communicate their message. Similar to the effects of line length, the presence of punctuation at the end of a line can create pauses that affect a reader's pace. **End-stopped** lines, or lines with a punctuation mark at the end, create a pause that can contribute to the poem's flow or create emphasis. **Enjambed** lines, or lines that do not end with a punctuation mark, carry a sentence to the next line and create an effect similar to long lines. The use of enjambment can speed up a poem's flow and reflect an idea within the poem or contribute to tone.

Quote and summarize Andrew Marvell's "To His Coy Mistress" and Robert Herrick's "To the Virgins, to Make Much of Time," briefly comparing and contrasting their treatments of *carpe diem* ("seize the day") tradition.

Discuss the effect a poem's structure has on the poem and its message.

Discuss how line length can impact both a poem's message and the reader's experience.

Define concrete poetry, or shape poetry, and discuss its effects on a poem.

Define free verse poetry and how it differs from other structures. Define enjambment and end-stopped lines and the effect that each has within a poem.

Give an example of how poetic structure enhances meaning in a poem via line length, punctuation, contradiction between the two, and meter.

Unlike prose, which traditionally (except in forms like stream of consciousness) consists of complete sentences connected into paragraphs, poetry is written in **verses**. These may form complete sentences, clauses, or phrases. Poetry may be written with or without rhyme. It can be metered, following a particular rhythmic pattern such as iambic, dactylic, spondaic, trochaic, or **anapestic**, or may be without regular meter. The terms **iamb** and **trochee**, among others, identify stressed and unstressed syllables in each verse. Meter is also described by the number of beats or stressed syllables per verse: **dimeter** (2), **trimeter** (3), **tetrameter** (4), **pentameter** (5), and so forth. Using the symbol ᴗ to denote unstressed and / to denote stressed syllables, **iambic** = ᴗ/; **trochaic** = /ᴗ; **spondaic** =//; **dactylic** =/ᴗᴗ; **anapestic** =ᴗᴗ/. **Rhyme schemes** identify which lines rhyme, such as ABAB, ABCA, AABA, and so on. Poetry with neither rhyme nor meter is called **free verse**. Poems may be in free verse, metered but unrhymed, rhymed but without meter, or using both rhyme and meter. In English, the most common meter is iambic pentameter. Unrhymed iambic pentameter is called **blank verse**.

Satire uses sarcasm, irony, and humor as social criticism to lampoon human folly. Unlike realism, which intends to depict reality as it exists without exaggeration, **satire** often involves creating situations or ideas that deliberately exaggerate reality to appear ridiculous to illuminate flawed behaviors. Ancient Roman satirists included Horace and Juvenal. Alexander Pope's poem "The Rape of the Lock" satirized the values of fashionable members of the 18th-century upper-middle class, which Pope found shallow and trivial. The theft of a lock of hair from a young woman is blown out of proportion: the poem's characters regard it as seriously as they would a rape. Irishman Jonathan Swift satirized British society, politics, and religion in works like "A Modest Proposal" and *Gulliver's Travels*. In "A Modest Proposal," Swift used essay form and mock-serious tone, satirically "proposing" cannibalism of babies and children as a solution to poverty and overpopulation. He satirized petty political disputes in *Gulliver's Travels*.

Haiku was originally a Japanese poetry form. In the 13th century, haiku was the opening phrase of renga, a 100-stanza oral poem. By the 16th century, haiku diverged into a separate short poem. When Western writers discovered haiku, the form became popular in English, as well as other languages. A haiku has 17 syllables, traditionally distributed across three lines as 5/7/5, with a pause after the first or second line. Haiku are syllabic and unrhymed. Haiku philosophy and technique are that brevity's compression forces writers to express images concisely, depict a moment in time, and evoke illumination and enlightenment. An example is 17th-century haiku master Matsuo Basho's classic: "An old silent pond.. / A frog jumps into the pond, / splash! Silence again." Modern American poet Ezra Pound revealed the influence of haiku in his two-line poem "In a Station of the Metro." In this poem, line 1 has 12 syllables (combining the syllable count of the first two lines of a haiku) and line 2 has 7, but it still preserves haiku's philosophy and imagistic technique: "The apparition of these faces in the crowd; / Petals on a wet, black bough."

From man's earliest days, he expressed himself with poetry. A large percentage of the surviving literature from ancient times is in **epic poetry**, utilized by Homer and other Greco-Roman poets. Epic poems typically recount heroic deeds and adventures, using stylized language and combining dramatic and lyrical conventions. **Epistolary poems**, poems that are written and read as letters, also developed in ancient times. In the fourteenth and fifteenth centuries, the **ballad** became a popular convention. Ballads often follow a rhyme scheme and meter and focus on subjects such as love, death, and religion. Many ballads tell stories, and several modern ballads are put to music. From these early conventions, numerous other poetic forms developed, such as **elegies**, **odes**, and **pastoral poems**. Elegies are mourning poems written in three parts: lament, praise of the deceased, and solace for loss. Odes evolved from songs to the typical poem of the Romantic time period, expressing strong feelings and contemplative thoughts. Pastoral poems idealize nature and country living. Poetry can also be used to make short, pithy statements. **Epigrams** (memorable rhymes with one or two lines) and **limericks** (two lines of iambic dimeter followed by two lines of iambic dimeter and another of iambic trimeter) are known for humor and wit.

Carpe diem is Latin for "seize the day." A long poetic tradition, it advocates making the most of time because it passes swiftly and life is short. It is found in multiple languages, including Latin, Torquato Tasso's Italian, Pierre de Ronsard's French, and Edmund Spenser's English, and is often used in seduction to argue for indulging in earthly pleasures. Roman poet Horace's Ode 1.11 tells a younger woman, Leuconoe, to enjoy the present, not worrying about inevitable aging. Two Renaissance Metaphysical Poets, Andrew Marvell and Robert Herrick, treated *carpe diem* more as a call to action. In "To His Coy Mistress," Marvell points out that time is fleeting, arguing for love, and concluding that because they cannot stop time, they may as well defy it, getting the most out of the short time they have. In "To the Virgins, to Make Much of Time," Herrick advises young women to take advantage of their good fortune in being young by getting married before they become too old to attract men and have babies.

The sonnet traditionally has 14 lines of iambic pentameter, tightly organized around a theme. The Petrarchan sonnet, named for 14th-century Italian poet Petrarch, has an eight-line stanza, the octave, and a six-line stanza, the sestet. There is a change or turn, known as the volta, between the eighth and ninth verses, setting up the sestet's answer or summary. The rhyme scheme is ABBA/ABBA/CDECDE or CDCDCD. The English or Shakespearean sonnet has three quatrains and one couplet, with the rhyme scheme ABAB/CDCD/EFEF/GG. This format better suits English, which has fewer rhymes than Italian. The final couplet often contrasts sharply with the preceding quatrains, as in Shakespeare's sonnets—for example, Sonnet 130, "My mistress' eyes are nothing like the sun…And yet, by heaven, I think my love as rare / As any she belied with false compare." Variations on the sonnet form include Edmund Spenser's Spenserian sonnet in the 16th century, John Milton's Miltonic sonnet in the 17th century, and sonnet sequences. Sonnet sequences are seen in works such as John Donne's *La Corona* and Elizabeth Barrett Browning's *Sonnets from the Portuguese*.

Reading
© Mometrix Media - flashcardsecrets.com/louisiana
English I

Describe some characteristics of satire as a literary form, including how it contrasts with realism. Give some examples of satirical literature.

Reading
© Mometrix Media - flashcardsecrets.com/louisiana
English I

Identify some typical characteristics of the literary genre of poetry, including how it differs from prose.

Reading
© Mometrix Media - flashcardsecrets.com/louisiana
English I

Describe some aspects of structure and content in some major forms of the literary genre of poetry.

Reading
© Mometrix Media - flashcardsecrets.com/louisiana
English I

Summarize some aspects of origin, structure, content, and technique of the haiku as a poetic form, including examples of an original haiku and a modern Western poem influenced by haiku.

Reading
© Mometrix Media - flashcardsecrets.com/louisiana
English I

Summarize some characteristics of the sonnet as a form of poetry, including brief histories and structures of two different types of sonnets and summaries of variations.

Reading
© Mometrix Media - flashcardsecrets.com/louisiana
English I

Discuss the *carpe diem* tradition in poetry, focusing on a few ancient Roman and Renaissance examples.

A **narrative** is any composition that tells a story. Narratives have characters, settings, and a structure. Narratives may be fiction or nonfiction stories and may follow a linear or nonlinear structure. The purpose of a narrative is generally to entertain, but nonfiction narratives can be informative, as well. Narratives also appear in a variety of structures and formats.

Biographies are books written about another person's life. Biographies can be valuable historical resources. Though they provide a narrow view of the relevant time period and culture, their specificity can also provide a unique context for that period or culture. Biographies, especially those whose subject was a well-known and influential figure, can provide a more complete picture of the figure's life or contributions. Biographies can also serve as a source of inspiration or communicate a moral because of their focus on one person over an extended period of time.

Myths that explain how the world works, its creation, and human behavior exist in most ancient cultures and continue to influence modern cultures. Myths are stories that are part of a certain **mythology**, such as Norse mythology. Myths are so influential that they have even inspired numerous pieces of modern literature and media in popular culture. While popular culture most clearly references myths from the Ancient Greek and Roman cultures, literature has been influenced by mythologies from around the entire world. Since myths are so prevalent in ancient literature, it makes sense that universal themes and morals often appear in mythologies from different cultures. The similarities and parallels (e.g., Greek myths about Zeus are very similar to Roman myths about Jupiter) suggest connections between cultures.

The **mystery** genre includes stories with plots that follow a protagonist as they work to solve an unexplained situation, such as a murder, disappearance, or robbery. Protagonists of mysteries may be hired professionals or amateurs who solve the mystery despite their lack of experience and resources. Mysteries allow the reader to solve the case along with the protagonist, and often grant the reader an advantageous perspective, creating dramatic irony. The *Sherlock Holmes* novels by Sir Arthur Conan Doyle are examples of mystery novels.

Science fiction is a genre that is based on the manipulation and exaggeration of real scientific discoveries and processes. These works are speculative and frequently depict a world where scientific discoveries and society have progressed beyond the point reached at the time of the work's creation. Works of science fiction often take place in a distant location or time, allowing for the dramatic advancements and conveniences they often depict. *Dune*, written by Frank Herbert, is an example of a science-fiction novel.

The **fantasy** genre includes stories that feature imaginary creatures and supernatural abilities, but often take place in settings that resemble real places and cultures in history. Fantasy novels usually follow a gifted protagonist from humble beginnings as they embark on a quest, journey, or adventure and encounter mystical beings and personally challenging obstacles. Common themes in the fantasy genre include personal growth, good versus evil, and the value of the journey. J.R.R. Tolkien's *The Lord of the Rings* trilogy belongs to the fantasy genre.

Realism is a literary form with the goal of representing reality as faithfully as possible. Its genesis in Western literature was a reaction against the sentimentality and extreme emotionalism of the works written during the Romantic literary movement, which championed feelings and emotional expression. Realists focused in great detail on immediacy of time and place, on specific actions of their characters, and the justifiable consequences of those actions. Some techniques of **realism** include writing in vernacular (conversational language), using specific dialects, and placing an emphasis on character rather than plot. Realistic literature also often addresses ethical issues. Historically, realistic works have often concentrated on the middle classes of the authors' societies. Realists eschew treatments that are too dramatic or sensationalistic as exaggerations of the reality that they strive to portray as closely as they are able. Influenced by his own bleak past, Fyodor Dostoevsky wrote several novels, such as *Crime and Punishment* (1866) that shunned romantic ideals and sought to portray a stark reality. Henry James was a prominent writer of realism in novels such as *Daisy Miller* (1879). Samuel Clemens (Mark Twain) skillfully represented the language and culture of lower-class Mississippi in his novel *The Adventures of Huckleberry Finn* (1885).

Roman à clef, French for "novel with a key," refers to books that require a real-life frame of reference, or key, for full comprehension. In Geoffrey Chaucer's *Canterbury Tales,* the Nun's Priest's Tale contains details that confuse readers unaware of history about the Earl of Bolingbroke's involvement in an assassination plot. Other literary works fitting this form include John Dryden's political satirical poem "Absalom and Achitophel" (1681), Jonathan Swift's satire "A Tale of a Tub" (1704), and George Orwell's political allegory *Animal Farm* (1945), all of which cannot be understood completely without knowing their camouflaged historical contents. *Roman à clefs* disguise truths too dangerous for authors to state directly. Readers must know about the enemies of D. H. Lawrence and Aldous Huxley to appreciate their respective novels: *Aaron's Rod* (1922) and *Point Counter Point* (1928). Marcel Proust's *Remembrance of Things Past (À la recherché du temps perdu,* 1871-1922) is informed by his social context. James Joyce's *Finnegans Wake* is an enormous *roman à clef* containing multitudinous personal references.

Folktales are stories that have withstood time and are usually popular in a particular region or culture. Folktales often depict the clever success of a common person, though the story may, alternatively, end poorly for the protagonist. A collection of folktales relevant to a particular region or culture is known as that culture's **folklore**. There are three common types of folktales: fables, fairy tales, and legends.

Fables are short, didactic stories that typically feature imaginary creatures or talking animals. The famous story "The Tortoise and the Hare" is a fable. Fables are still told and used today because of their universally understandable morals and characters, which also make them suitable for children's literature and media.

Fairy tales are stories that involve fictional creatures or realistic characters with fantastical traits and abilities. Fairy tales often end happily and depict the victory of good over evil. The plots and characters in fairy tales are often far-fetched and whimsical.

Legends are stories that typically focus on one character and highlight their victory over a particular enemy or obstacle. Legends often feature some facts or are inspired by true events, but are generally considered both unproven and unprovable. Heroes are often the protagonists of legends, and they generally save or protect others as they conquer enemies and obstacles.

A **short story** is a fictional narrative that is shorter than a novel. However, there is not a definite page or word count that defines the short story category. Short stories tend to focus on one or few elements of a story in order to efficiently tell the story. Though they are often brief, short stories may still contain a moral or impact their readers.

Realistic fiction describes fictional narratives that include events and characters that do not exist, but could appear in reality. Within the narrative, these characters and events may be depicted in real places. For example, Pip, the protagonist of Charles Dickens's *Great Expectations*, was not a real person, but the novel shows him living in London, England for much of his young adulthood. Realistic fiction contains no far-fetched or impossible elements and presents situations that can or do occur in real life. A contemporary example of realistic fiction is *Wonder* by R.J. Palacio.

Historical fiction includes works that take place in the past and model their setting after real historical cultures, societies, and time periods. These works may include real historical figures and events, but they also may not. Works of historical fiction must be fully informed by the period and location they are set in, meaning both the major and minor details of the work must be historically compatible with the work's setting. Examples of historical fiction include Kathryn Stockett's *The Help* and Markus Zusak's *The Book Thief*.

The phrase **literary nonfiction** describes nonfiction narratives that present true facts and events in a way that entertains readers and displays creativity. Literary nonfiction, also called creative nonfiction, may resemble fiction in its style and flow, but the truth of the events it describes sets it apart from fictional literature. Different types of books may be considered literary nonfiction, such as biographies, if they appear to employ creativity in their writing. An example of literary nonfiction is *The Immortal Life of Henrietta Lacks* by Rebecca Skloot.

Reading
© Mometrix Media - flashcardsecrets.com/louisiana
English I

Define the *roman à clef*, giving examples of novels and other literary works fitting this form.

Reading
© Mometrix Media - flashcardsecrets.com/louisiana
English I

Define narratives, biographies, and myths.

Reading
© Mometrix Media - flashcardsecrets.com/louisiana
English I

Define folktales, fables, fairy tales, legends, and short stories.

Visit *mometrix.com/academy* for a related video.
Enter video code: 347199

Reading
© Mometrix Media - flashcardsecrets.com/louisiana
English I

Define the mystery, science-fiction, and fantasy genres.

Reading
© Mometrix Media - flashcardsecrets.com/louisiana
English I

Define realistic fiction, historical fiction, and literary nonfiction.

Reading
© Mometrix Media - flashcardsecrets.com/louisiana
English I

Define realism as a literary form, including its main characteristics and genesis in Western literature.

Novels of manners are fictional stories that observe, explore, and analyze the social behaviors of a specific time and place. While deep psychological themes are more universal across different periods and countries, the manners of a particular society are shorter-lived and more varied; the **novel of manners** captures these societal details. Novels of manners can also be regarded as symbolically representing, in artistic form, certain established and secure social orders. Characteristics of novels of manners include descriptions of a society with defined behavioral codes; language that uses standardized, impersonal formulas; and inhibition of emotional expression, as contrasted with the strong emotions expressed in romantic or sentimental novels. Jane Austen's detailed descriptions of English society and characters struggling with the definitions and restrictions placed on them by society are excellent models of the novel of manners. In the 20th century, Evelyn Waugh's *Handful of Dust* is a novel of social manners, and his *Sword of Honour* trilogy contains novels of military manners. Another 20th-century example is *The Unbearable Bassington* by Saki (the pen name of writer H. H. Munro), focusing on Edwardian society.

Historical fiction is set in particular historical periods, including prehistoric and mythological. Examples include Walter Scott's *Rob Roy* and *Ivanhoe*; Leo Tolstoy's *War and Peace*; Robert Graves' *I, Claudius*; Mary Renault's *The King Must Die* and *The Bull from the Sea* (an historical novel using Greek mythology); Virginia Woolf's *Orlando* and *Between the Acts;* and John Dos Passos's *USA* trilogy. **Picaresque** novels recount episodic adventures of a rogue protagonist or *pícaro,* like Miguel de Cervantes' *Don Quixote* or Henry Fielding's *Tom Jones.* **Gothic** novels originated as a reaction against 18th-century Enlightenment rationalism, featuring horror, mystery, superstition, madness, supernatural elements, and revenge. Early examples include Horace Walpole's *Castle of Otranto,* Matthew Gregory Lewis' *Monk,* Mary Shelley's *Frankenstein*, and Bram Stoker's *Dracula.* In America, Edgar Allan Poe wrote many Gothic works. Contemporary novelist Anne Rice has penned many Gothic novels under the pseudonym A. N. Roquelaure. **Psychological** novels, originating in 17th-century France, explore characters' motivations. Examples include Abbé Prévost's *Manon Lescaut;* George Eliot's novels; Fyodor Dostoyevsky's *Crime and Punishment;* Tolstoy's *Anna Karenina;* Gustave Flaubert's *Madame Bovary;* and the novels of Henry James, James Joyce, and Vladimir Nabokov.

Epistolary novels are told in the form of letters written by their characters rather than in typical narrative form. Samuel Richardson, the best-known author of epistolary novels like *Pamela* (1740) and *Clarissa* (1748), widely influenced early Romantic epistolary novels throughout Europe that freely expressed emotions. Richardson, a printer, published technical manuals on letter-writing for young gentlewomen; his epistolary novels were fictional extensions of those nonfictional instructional books. Nineteenth-century English author Wilkie Collins' *The Moonstone* (1868) was a mystery written in epistolary form. By the 20th century, the format of well-composed written letters came to be regarded as artificial and outmoded. A 20th-century evolution of letters was tape-recording transcripts, such as in Irish playwright Samuel Beckett's drama *Krapp's Last Tape.* Though evoking modern alienation, Beckett still created a sense of fictional characters' direct communication without author intervention as Richardson had.

Sentimental love novels originated in the movement of Romanticism. Eighteenth-century examples of novels that emphasize the emotional aspect of love include Samuel Richardson's *Pamela* (1740) and Jean-Jacques Rousseau's *Nouvelle Héloïse* (1761). Also in the 18th century, Laurence Sterne's novel *Tristram Shandy* (1760-1767) is an example of a novel with elements of sentimentality. The Victorian era's rejection of emotionalism caused the term "sentimental" to have undesirable connotations. However, even non-sentimental novelists such as William Makepeace Thackeray and Charles Dickens incorporated sentimental elements in their writing. A 19th-century author of genuinely sentimental novels was Mrs. Henry Wood (e.g., *East Lynne,* 1861). In the 20th century, Erich Segal's sentimental novel *Love Story* (1970) was a popular bestseller.

Bildungsroman is German for "education novel." This term is also used in English to describe "apprenticeship" novels focusing on coming-of-age stories, including youth's struggles and searches for things such as identity, spiritual understanding, or the meaning in life. Johann Wolfgang von Goethe's *Wilhelm Meisters Lehrjahre* (1796) is credited as the origin of this genre. Two of Charles Dickens' novels, *David Copperfield* (1850) and *Great Expectations* (1861), also fit this form. H. G. Wells wrote *bildungsromans* about questing for apprenticeships to address the complications of modern life in *Joan and Peter* (1918) and from a Utopian perspective in *The Dream* (1924). School *bildungsromans* include Thomas Hughes' *Tom Brown's School Days* (1857) and Alain-Fournier's *Le Grand Meaulnes* (1913). Many Hermann Hesse novels, including *Demian, Steppenwolf, Siddhartha, Magister Ludi,* and *Beneath the Wheel* are *bildungsromans* about a struggling, searching youth. Samuel Butler's *The Way of All Flesh* (1903) and James Joyce's *A Portrait of the Artist as a Young Man* (1916) are two modern examples. Variations include J. D. Salinger's *The Catcher in the Rye* (1951), set both within and beyond school, and William Golding's *Lord of the Flies* (1955), a novel not set in a school but one that is a coming-of-age story nonetheless.

Pastoral novels lyrically idealize country life as idyllic and utopian, akin to the Garden of Eden. *Daphnis and Chloe*, written by Greek novelist Longus around the second or third century, influenced Elizabethan pastoral romances like Thomas Lodge's *Rosalynde* (1590), which inspired Shakespeare's *As You Like It*, and Philip Sidney's *Arcadia* (1590). Jacques-Henri Bernardin de St. Pierre's French work *Paul et Virginie* (1787) demonstrated the early Romantic view of the innocence and goodness of nature. Though the style lost popularity by the 20th century, pastoral elements can still be seen in novels like *The Rainbow* (1915) and *Lady Chatterley's Lover* (1928), both by D. H. Lawrence. Growing realism transformed pastoral writing into less ideal and more dystopian, distasteful and ironic depictions of country life in George Eliot's and Thomas Hardy's novels. Saul Bellow's novel *Herzog* (1964) may demonstrate how urban ills highlight an alternative pastoral ideal. The pastoral style is commonly thought to be overly idealized and outdated today, as seen in Stella Gibbons' pastoral satire, Cold Comfort Farm (1932).

Identify some elements and examples of four major forms of the literary genre of novels.

Discuss some aspects that define the novel of manners, including some examples.

Summarize the origin of Western-world sentimental novels. Give some examples of sentimental novels and novels containing sentimental elements.

Define the epistolary novel as one form of the genre. Give some examples of 18th- and 19th-century epistolary novels. Identify a 20th-century attempt to revive this form and the outcome.

Define pastoral novels as a form of the genre. Identify ancient influences, including an example. Give some examples of earlier and later Western works with pastoral influences, and discuss the influences that changed pastoral literature.

Translate *bildungsroman* and explain what form it is in the genre of novels. Give some examples, including variations.

First-person narratives let narrators express inner feelings and thoughts, especially when the narrator is the protagonist as Lemuel Gulliver is in Jonathan Swift's *Gulliver's Travels*. The narrator may be a close friend of the protagonist, like Dr. Watson in Sir Arthur Conan Doyle's *Sherlock Holmes*. Or, the narrator can be less involved with the main characters and plot, like Nick Carraway in F. Scott Fitzgerald's *The Great Gatsby*. When a narrator reports others' narratives, she or he is a "**frame narrator**," like the nameless narrator of Joseph Conrad's *Heart of Darkness* or Mr. Lockwood in Emily Brontë's *Wuthering Heights*. **First-person plural** is unusual but can be effective. Isaac Asimov's *I, Robot*, William Faulkner's *A Rose for Emily*, Maxim Gorky's *Twenty-Six Men and a Girl*, and Jeffrey Eugenides' *The Virgin Suicides* all use first-person plural narration. Author Kurt Vonnegut is the first-person narrator in his semi-autobiographical novel *Timequake*. Also unusual, but effective, is a **first-person omniscient** (rather than the more common third-person omniscient) narrator, like Death in Markus Zusak's *The Book Thief* and the ghost in Alice Sebold's *The Lovely Bones*.

Another element that impacts a text is the author's point of view. The **point of view** of a text is the perspective from which a passage is told. An author will always have a point of view about a story before he or she draws up a plot line. The author will know what events they want to take place, how they want the characters to interact, and how they want the story to resolve. An author will also have an opinion on the topic or series of events which is presented in the story that is based on their prior experience and beliefs.

The two main points of view that authors use, especially in a work of fiction, are first person and third person. If the narrator of the story is also the main character, or *protagonist*, the text is written in first-person point of view. In first person, the author writes from the perspective of *I*. Third-person point of view is probably the most common that authors use in their passages. Using third person, authors refer to each character by using *he* or *she*. In third-person omniscient, the narrator is not a character in the story and tells the story of all of the characters at the same time.

Narration in the third person is the most prevalent type, as it allows authors the most flexibility. It is so common that readers simply assume without needing to be informed that the narrator is not a character in the story, or involved in its events. **Third-person singular** is used more frequently than **third-person plural**, though some authors have also effectively used plural. However, both singular and plural are most often included in stories according to which characters are being described. The third-person narrator may be either objective or subjective, and either omniscient or limited. **Objective third-person** narration does not include what the characters described are thinking or feeling, while **subjective third-person** narration does. The **third-person omniscient** narrator knows everything about all characters, including their thoughts and emotions, and all related places, times, and events. However, the **third-person limited** narrator may know everything about a particular character, but is limited to that character. In other words, the narrator cannot speak about anything that character does not know.

While **second-person** address is very commonplace in popular song lyrics, it is the least used form of narrative voice in literary works. Popular serial books of the 1980s like *Fighting Fantasy* or *Choose Your Own Adventure* employed second-person narratives. In some cases, a narrative combines both second-person and first-person voices, using the pronouns *you* and *I*. This can draw readers into the story, and it can also enable the authors to compare directly "your" and "my" feelings, thoughts, and actions. When the narrator is also a character in the story, as in Edgar Allan Poe's short story "The Tell-Tale Heart" or Jay McInerney's novel *Bright Lights, Big City*, the narrative is better defined as first-person despite its also addressing "you."

Fiction that is heavily influenced by a historical or social context cannot be comprehended as the author intended if the reader does not keep this context in mind. Many important elements of the text will be influenced by any context, including symbols, allusions, settings, and plot events. These contexts, as well as the identity of the work's author, can help to inform the reader about the author's concerns and intended meanings. For example, George Orwell published his novel *1984* in the year 1949, soon after the end of World War II. At that time, following the defeat of the Nazis, the Cold War began between the Western Allied nations and the Eastern Soviet Communists. People were therefore concerned about the conflict between the freedoms afforded by Western democracies versus the oppression represented by Communism. Orwell had also previously fought in the Spanish Civil War against a Spanish regime that he and his fellows viewed as oppressive. From this information, readers can infer that Orwell was concerned about oppression by totalitarian governments. This informs *1984*'s story of Winston Smith's rebellion against the oppressive "Big Brother" government, of the fictional dictatorial state of Oceania, and his capture, torture, and ultimate conversion by that government. Some literary theories also seek to use historical and social contexts to reveal deeper meanings and implications in a text.

Although authors more commonly write stories from one point of view, there are also instances wherein they alternate the narrative voice within the same book. For example, they may sometimes use an omniscient third-person narrator and a more intimate first-person narrator at other times. In J. K. Rowling's series of *Harry Potter* novels, she often writes in a third-person limited narrative, but sometimes changes to narration by characters other than the protagonist. George R. R. Martin's series *A Song of Ice and Fire* changes the point of view to coincide with divisions between chapters. The same technique is used by Erin Hunter (a pseudonym for several authors of the *Warriors, Seekers,* and *Survivors* book series). Authors using first-person narrative sometimes switch to third-person to describe significant action scenes, especially those where the narrator was absent or uninvolved, as Barbara Kingsolver does in her novel *The Poisonwood Bible*.

Reading
© Mometrix Media - flashcardsecrets.com/louisiana
English I

Explain point of view.

Reading
© Mometrix Media - flashcardsecrets.com/louisiana
English I

Identify some different types of first-person narration in literature, giving examples of each.

Reading
© Mometrix Media - flashcardsecrets.com/louisiana
English I

Discuss some characteristics and examples of the second-person type of narrative in literature.

Reading
© Mometrix Media - flashcardsecrets.com/louisiana
English I

Describe some distinctive features of third-person narrative as it is used in literature.

Reading
© Mometrix Media - flashcardsecrets.com/louisiana
English I

Identify some characteristics and examples of the alternating-person narrative in literature.

Reading
© Mometrix Media - flashcardsecrets.com/louisiana
English I

Discuss the impact that historical and social contexts can have on a fictional text's meaning. Give an example of a novel that is heavily informed by social and historical contexts.

A well-known example of character development can be found in Charles Dickens's *Great Expectations*. The novel's main character, Pip, is introduced as a young boy, and he is depicted as innocent, kind, and humble. However, as Pip grows up and is confronted with the social hierarchy of Victorian England, he becomes arrogant and rejects his loved ones in pursuit of his own social advancement. Once he achieves his social goals, he realizes the merits of his former lifestyle, and lives with the wisdom he gained in both environments and life stages. Dickens shows Pip's ever-changing character through his interactions with others and his inner thoughts, which evolve as his personal values and personality shift.

When depicting characters or figures in a written text, authors generally use actions, dialogue, and descriptions as characterization techniques. Characterization can occur in both fiction and nonfiction and is used to show a character or figure's personality, demeanor, and thoughts. This helps create a more engaging experience for the reader by providing a more concrete picture of a character or figure's tendencies and features. Characterizations also gives authors the opportunity to integrate elements such as dialects, activities, attire, and attitudes into their writing.

To understand the meaning of a story, it is vital to understand the characters as the author describes them. We can look for contradictions in what a character thinks, says, and does. We can notice whether the author's observations about a character differ from what other characters in the story say about that character. A character may be dynamic, meaning they change significantly during the story, or static, meaning they remain the same from beginning to end. Characters may be two-dimensional, not fully developed, or may be well developed with characteristics that stand out vividly. Characters may also symbolize universal properties. Additionally, readers can compare and contrast characters to analyze how each one developed.

In fictional works, effectively written dialogue does more than just break up or interrupt sections of narrative. While dialogue may supply exposition for readers, it must nonetheless be believable. Dialogue should be dynamic, not static, and it should not resemble regular prose. Authors should not use dialogue to write clever similes or metaphors, or to inject their own opinions. Nor should they use dialogue at all when narrative would be better. Most importantly, dialogue should not slow the plot movement. Dialogue must seem natural, which means careful construction of phrases rather than actually duplicating natural speech, which does not necessarily translate well to the written word. Finally, all dialogue must be pertinent to the story, rather than just added conversation.

Effectively written **dialogue** serves at least one, but usually several, purposes. It advances the story and moves the plot, develops the characters, sheds light on the work's theme or meaning, and can, often subtly, account for the passage of time not otherwise indicated. It can alter the direction that the plot is taking, typically by introducing some new conflict or changing existing ones. Dialogue can establish a work's narrative voice and the characters' voices and set the tone of the story or of particular characters. When fictional characters display enlightenment or realization, dialogue can give readers an understanding of what those characters have discovered and how. Dialogue can illuminate the motivations and wishes of the story's characters. By using consistent thoughts and syntax, dialogue can support character development. Skillfully created, it can also represent real-life speech rhythms in written form. Via conflicts and ensuing action, dialogue also provides drama.

Symbolism describes an author's use of a **symbol**, an element of the story that **represents** something else. Symbols can impact stories in many ways, including deepening the meaning of a story or its elements, comparing a story to another work, or foreshadowing later events in a story. Symbols can be objects, characters, colors, numbers, or anything else the author establishes as a symbol. Symbols can be clearly established through direct comparison or repetition, but they can also be established subtly or gradually over a large portion of the story. Another form of symbolism is **allusion**, which is when something in a story is used to prompt the reader to think about another work. Many well-known works use **Biblical allusions**, which are allusions to events or details in the Bible that inform a work or an element within it.

Foreshadowing is a device authors use to give readers **hints** about events that will take place later in a story. Foreshadowing most often takes place through a character's dialogue or actions. Sometimes the character will know what is going to happen and will purposefully allude to future events. For example, consider a protagonist who is about to embark on a journey through the woods. Just before the protagonist begins the trip, another character says, "Be careful, you never know what could be out in those woods!" This alerts the reader that the woods may be dangerous and prompts the reader to expect something to attack the protagonist in the woods. This is an example of foreshadowing through warning. Alternatively, a character may unknowingly foreshadow later events. For example, consider a story where a brother and sister run through their house and knock over a vase and break it. The brother says, "Don't worry, we'll clean it up! Mom will never know!" However, the reader knows that their mother will most likely find out what they have done, so the reader expects the siblings to later get in trouble for running, breaking the vase, and hiding it from their mother.

Reading
© Mometrix Media - flashcardsecrets.com/louisiana
English I

Define characterization and discuss how it affects the plot and meaning of a story.

Reading
© Mometrix Media - flashcardsecrets.com/louisiana
English I

Discuss a real example of characterization in classic literature and how it is shown in the work.

Reading
© Mometrix Media - flashcardsecrets.com/louisiana
English I

Relate a number of purposes that good dialogue serves in literary fiction.

Reading
© Mometrix Media - flashcardsecrets.com/louisiana
English I

Describe a number of things that good dialogue in fictional literary works virtually never does, or should not do.

Reading
© Mometrix Media - flashcardsecrets.com/louisiana
English I

Define foreshadowing and give some examples of common methods of foreshadowing.

Reading
© Mometrix Media - flashcardsecrets.com/louisiana
English I

Define symbolism and discuss some ways authors establish and use symbols in literature.

An allusion is an uncited but recognizable reference to something else. Authors use language to make allusions to places, events, artwork, and other books in order to make their own text richer. For example, an author may allude to a very important text in order to make his own text seem more important. Martin Luther King, Jr. started his "I Have a Dream" speech by saying "Five score years ago..." This is a clear allusion to President Abraham Lincoln's "Gettysburg Address" and served to remind people of the significance of the event. An author may allude to a place to ground his text or make a cultural reference to make readers feel included. There are many reasons that authors make allusions.

Mood is a story's atmosphere, or the feelings the reader gets from reading it. The way authors set the mood in writing is comparable to the way filmmakers use music to set the mood in movies. Instead of music, though, writers judiciously select descriptive words to evoke certain **moods**. The mood of a work may convey joy, anger, bitterness, hope, gloom, fear, apprehension, or any other emotion the author wants the reader to feel. In addition to vocabulary choices, authors also use figurative expressions, particular sentence structures, and choices of diction that project and reinforce the moods they want to create. Whereas mood is the reader's emotions evoked by reading what is written, **tone** is the emotions and attitudes of the writer that she or he expresses in the writing. Authors use the same literary techniques to establish tone as they do to establish mood. An author may use a humorous tone, an angry or sad tone, a sentimental or unsentimental tone, or something else entirely.

To understand the difference between mood and tone, look at this excerpt from F. Scott Fitzgerald's *The Great Gatsby*. In this passage, Nick Caraway, the novel's narrator, is describing his affordable house, which sits in a neighborhood full of expensive mansions.

> *I lived at West Egg, the—well the less fashionable of the two, though this is a most superficial tag to express the bizarre and not a little sinister contrast between them. My house was at the very tip of the egg, only fifty yard from the Sound, and squeezed between two huge places that rented for twelve or fifteen thousand a season ... My own house was an eyesore, but it was a small eyesore, and it had been overlooked, so I had a view of the water, a partial view of my neighbor's lawn, and the consoling proximity of millionaires—all for eighty dollars a month.*

Fitzgerald conveys an attitude, or tone, through Nick's description that does not align with the passage's mood. Nick calls the distinction between the neighborhoods "superficial," showing a suspicion of the value suggested by the neighborhoods' titles, properties, and residents. Nick also undermines his critique of his own home by calling it "a small eyesore" and claiming it has "been overlooked." However, he follows these statements with a description of his surroundings, claiming that he has "a view of the water" and can see some of his wealthy neighbor's property from his home, and a comparison between the properties' rent. While the mental image created for the reader depicts a small house shoved between looming mansions, the tone suggests that Nick enjoys these qualities about his home, or at least finds it charming. He acknowledges its shortcomings, but includes the benefits of his home's unassuming appearance.

Authors use words and **syntax**, or sentence structure, to make their texts unique, convey their own writing style, and sometimes to make a point or emphasis. They know that word choice and syntax contribute to the reader's understanding of the text as well as to the tone and mood of a text.

Comic relief is the use of comedy by an author to break up a dramatic or tragic scene and infuse it with a bit of **lightheartedness**. In William Shakespeare's *Hamlet*, two gravediggers digging the grave for Ophelia share a joke while they work. The death and burial of Ophelia are tragic moments that directly follow each other. Shakespeare uses an instance of comedy to break up the tragedy and give his audience a bit of a break from the tragic drama. Authors sometimes use comic relief so that their work will be less depressing; other times they use it to create irony or contrast between the darkness of the situation and the lightness of the joke. Often, authors will use comedy to parallel what is happening in the tragic scenes.

To understand the difference between mood and tone, look at this excerpt from F. Scott Fitzgerald's *The Great Gatsby*. In this passage, Nick Caraway, the novel's narrator, is describing his affordable house, which sits in a neighborhood full of expensive mansions.

> *I lived at West Egg, the—well the less fashionable of the two, though this is a most superficial tag to express the bizarre and not a little sinister contrast between them. My house was at the very tip of the egg, only fifty yard from the Sound, and squeezed between two huge places that rented for twelve or fifteen thousand a season ... My own house was an eyesore, but it was a small eyesore, and it had been overlooked, so I had a view of the water, a partial view of my neighbor's lawn, and the consoling proximity of millionaires—all for eighty dollars a month.*

In this description, the mood created for the reader does not match the tone created through the narrator. The mood in this passage is one of dissatisfaction and inferiority. Nick compares his home to his neighbors', saying he lives in the "less fashionable" neighborhood and that his house is "overlooked," an "eyesore," and "squeezed between two huge" mansions. He also adds that his placement allows him the "consoling proximity of millionaires." A literal reading of these details leads the reader to have negative feelings toward Nick's house and his economic inferiority to his neighbors, creating the mood.

Reading
© Mometrix Media - flashcardsecrets.com/louisiana
English I

Discuss the importance of syntax.

Reading
© Mometrix Media - flashcardsecrets.com/louisiana
English I

Discuss how the use of allusion affects both a text and the audience.

Reading
© Mometrix Media - flashcardsecrets.com/louisiana
English I

Describe the use of comic relief.

Reading
© Mometrix Media - flashcardsecrets.com/louisiana
English I

Define mood and tone in literature. Explain how authors create a tone and mood for a story.

Reading
© Mometrix Media - flashcardsecrets.com/louisiana
English I

Understand the difference between mood and tone. Describe the mood that is communicated after reading an excerpt.

Reading
© Mometrix Media - flashcardsecrets.com/louisiana
English I

Understand the difference between mood and tone. Describe the tone that is communicated after reading an excerpt.

A **conflict** is a problem to be solved. Literary plots typically include one conflict or more. Characters' attempts to resolve conflicts drive the narrative's forward movement. **Conflict resolution** is often the protagonist's primary occupation. Physical conflicts like exploring, wars, and escapes tend to make plots most suspenseful and exciting. Emotional, mental, or moral conflicts tend to make stories more personally gratifying or rewarding for many audiences. Conflicts can be external or internal. A major type of internal conflict is some inner personal battle, or **man versus self**. Major types of external conflicts include **man versus nature**, **man versus man**, and **man versus society**. Readers can identify conflicts in literary plots by identifying the protagonist and antagonist and asking why they conflict, what events develop the conflict, where the climax occurs, and how they identify with the characters.

Read the following paragraph and discuss the type of conflict present:

Timothy was shocked out of sleep by the appearance of a bear just outside his tent. After panicking for a moment, he remembered some advice he had read in preparation for this trip: he should make noise so the bear would not be startled. As Timothy started to hum and sing, the bear wandered away.

There are three main types of conflict in literature: **man versus man**, **man versus nature**, and **man versus self**. This paragraph is an example of man versus nature. Timothy is in conflict with the bear. Even though no physical conflict like an attack exists, Timothy is pitted against the bear. Timothy uses his knowledge to "defeat" the bear and keep himself safe. The solution to the conflict is that Timothy makes noise, the bear wanders away, and Timothy is safe.

The **exposition** is at the beginning of the story and generally takes place before the rising action begins. The purpose of the exposition is to give the reader context for the story, which the author may do by introducing one or more characters, describing the setting or world, or explaining the events leading up to the point where the story begins. The exposition may still include events that contribute to the plot, but the **rising action** and main conflict of the story are not part of the exposition. Some narratives skip the exposition and begin the story with the beginning of the rising action, which causes the reader to learn the context as the story intensifies.

The **climax** is the event in the narrative that marks the height of the story's conflict or tension. The event that takes place at the story's climax will end the rising action and bring about the results of the main conflict. If the conflict was between a good protagonist and an evil antagonist, the climax may be a final battle between the two characters. If the conflict is an adventurer looking for heavily guarded treasure, the climax may be the adventurer's encounter with the final obstacle that protects the treasure. The climax may be made of multiple scenes, but can usually be summarized as one event. Once the conflict and climax are complete, the **falling action** begins.

The **rising action** is the part of the story where conflict **intensifies**. The rising action begins with an event that prompts the main conflict of the story. This may also be called the **inciting incident**. The main conflict generally occurs between the protagonist and an antagonist, but this is not the only type of conflict that may occur in a narrative. After this event, the protagonist works to resolve the main conflict by preparing for an altercation, pursuing a goal, fleeing an antagonist, or doing some other action that will end the conflict. The rising action is composed of several additional events that increase the story's tension. Most often, other developments will occur alongside the growth of the main conflict, such as character development or the development of minor conflicts. The rising action ends with the **climax**, which is the point of highest tension in the story.

The way the conflict is **resolved** depends on the type of conflict. The plot of any book starts with the lead up to the conflict, then the conflict itself, and finally the solution, or **resolution**, to the conflict. In **man versus man** conflicts, the conflict is often resolved by two parties coming to some sort of agreement or by one party triumphing over the other party. In **man versus nature** conflicts, the conflict is often resolved by man coming to some realization about some aspect of nature. In **man versus self** conflicts, the conflict is often resolved by the character growing or coming to an understanding about part of himself.

The **falling action** shows what happens in the story between the climax and the resolution. The falling action often composes a much smaller portion of the story than the rising action does. While the climax includes the end of the main conflict, the falling action may show the results of any minor conflicts in the story. For example, if the protagonist encountered a troll on the way to find some treasure, and the troll demanded the protagonist share the treasure after retrieving it, the falling action would include the protagonist returning to share the treasure with the troll. Similarly, any unexplained major events are usually made clear during the falling action. Once all significant elements of the story are resolved or addressed, the story's resolution will occur. The **resolution** is the end of the story, which shows the final result of the plot's events and shows what life is like for the main characters once they are no longer experiencing the story's conflicts.

Reading
© Mometrix Media - flashcardsecrets.com/louisiana
English I

Describe the exposition component of basic plot structure.

Reading
© Mometrix Media - flashcardsecrets.com/louisiana
English I

Define conflict relative to literary plot. Identify some major kinds of plot conflicts. Articulate some ways the reader can identify conflict in a literary plot.

Visit *mometrix.com/academy* for a related video.
Enter video code: 559550

Reading
© Mometrix Media - flashcardsecrets.com/louisiana
English I

Describe the rising action component of basic plot structure.

Reading
© Mometrix Media - flashcardsecrets.com/louisiana
English I

Describe the climax component of basic plot structure.

Reading
© Mometrix Media - flashcardsecrets.com/louisiana
English I

Describe the falling action and resolution components of basic plot structure.

Reading
© Mometrix Media - flashcardsecrets.com/louisiana
English I

Describe how the type of conflict found in a text influences the resolution.

A literary text has both a setting and time frame. A **setting** is the place in which the story as a whole is set. The **time frame** is the period in which the story is set. This may refer to the historical period the story takes place in or if the story takes place over a single day. Both setting and time frame are relevant to a text's meaning because they help the reader place the story in time and space. An author uses setting and time frame to anchor a text, create a mood, and enhance its meaning. This helps a reader understand why a character acts the way he does, or why certain events in the story are important. The setting impacts the **plot** and character **motivations**, while the time frame helps place the story in **chronological context**.

A **theme** is a central idea demonstrated by a passage. Often, a theme is a lesson or moral contained in the text, but it does not have to be. It also is a unifying idea that is used throughout the text; it can take the form of a common setting, idea, symbol, design, or recurring event. A passage can have two or more themes that convey its overall idea. The theme or themes of a passage are often based on **universal themes**. They can frequently be expressed using well-known sayings about life, society, or human nature, such as "Hard work pays off" or "Good triumphs over evil." Themes are not usually stated **explicitly**. The reader must figure them out by carefully reading the passage. Themes are created through descriptive language or events in the plot. The events of a story help shape the themes of a passage.

The **plot** includes the events that happen in a story and the order in which they are told to the reader. There are several types of plot structures, as stories can be told in many ways. The most common plot structure is the chronological plot, which presents the events to the reader in the same order they occur for the characters in the story. Chronological plots usually have five main parts, the **exposition**, **rising action**, the **climax**, **falling action**, and the **resolution**. This type of plot structure guides the reader through the story's events as the characters experience them and is the easiest structure to understand and identify. While this is the most common plot structure, many stories are nonlinear, which means the plot does not sequence events in the same order the characters experience them. Such stories might include elements like flashbacks that cause the story to be nonlinear.

Idioms create comparisons, and often take the form of similes or metaphors. Idioms are always phrases and are understood to have a meaning that is different from its individual words' literal meaning. For example, "break a leg" is a common idiom that is used to wish someone luck or tell them to perform well. Literally, the phrase "break a leg" means to injure a person's leg, but the phrase takes on a different meaning when used as an idiom. Another example is "call it a day," which means to temporarily stop working on a task, or find a stopping point, rather than literally referring to something as "a day." Many idioms are associated with a region or group. For example, an idiom commonly used in the American South is "'til the cows come home." This phrase is often used to indicate that something will take or may last for a very long time, but not that it will literally last until the cows return to where they reside.

Read the following excerpt from The Adventures of Huckleberry Finn by Mark Twain and analyze the relevance of setting to the text's meaning:

> *We said there warn't no home like a raft, after all. Other places do seem so cramped up and smothery, but a raft don't. You feel mighty free and easy and comfortable on a raft.*

This excerpt from The Adventures of Huckleberry Finn by Mark Twain reveals information about the **setting** of the book. By understanding that the main character, Huckleberry Finn, lives on a raft, the reader can place the story on a river, in this case, the Mississippi River in the South before the Civil War. The information about the setting also gives the reader clues about the **character** of Huck Finn: he clearly values independence and freedom, and he likes the outdoors. The information about the setting in the quote helps the reader to better understand the rest of the text.

Explain why "if you care about something, you need to take care of it" accurately describes the theme of the following excerpt.

> *Luca collected baseball cards, but he wasn't very careful with them. He left them around the house. His dog liked to chew. One day, Luca and his friend Bart were looking at his collection. Then they went outside. When Luca got home, he saw his dog chewing on his cards. They were ruined.*

This excerpt tells the story of a boy who is careless with his baseball cards and leaves them lying around. His dog ends up chewing them and ruining them. The lesson is that if you care about something, you need to take care of it. This is the theme, or point, of the story. Some stories have more than one theme, but this is not really true of this excerpt. The reader needs to figure out the theme based on what happens in the story. Sometimes, as in the case of fables, the theme is stated directly in the text. However, this is not usually the case.

Reading
© Mometrix Media - flashcardsecrets.com/louisiana
English I

Define idioms and identify the meanings of common idioms.

Reading
© Mometrix Media - flashcardsecrets.com/louisiana
English I

Describe the influence of setting in literary texts.

Reading
© Mometrix Media - flashcardsecrets.com/louisiana
English I

Describe how a brief passage can reveal information about the setting and its significance in the text.

Reading
© Mometrix Media - flashcardsecrets.com/louisiana
English I

Discuss how to determine the theme of a text, as well as how theme contributes to meaning.

Reading
© Mometrix Media - flashcardsecrets.com/louisiana
English I

Discuss how theme can be identified in a text.

Reading
© Mometrix Media - flashcardsecrets.com/louisiana
English I

Define plot, the components of basic plot structure, and nonlinear plots.

A **metaphor** is a type of figurative language in which the writer equates something with another thing that is not particularly similar, instead of using *like* or *as*. For instance, *the bird was an arrow arcing through the sky*. In this sentence, the arrow is serving as a metaphor for the bird. The point of a metaphor is to encourage the reader to consider the item being described in a *different way*. Let's continue with this metaphor for a flying bird. You are asked to envision the bird's flight as being similar to the arc of an arrow. So, you imagine the flight to be swift and bending. Metaphors are a way for the author to describe an item *without being direct and obvious*. This literary device is a lyrical and suggestive way of providing information. Note that the reference for a metaphor will not always be mentioned explicitly by the author. Consider the following description of a forest in winter: *Swaying skeletons reached for the sky and groaned as the wind blew through them.* In this example, the author is using *skeletons* as a metaphor for leafless trees. This metaphor creates a spooky tone while inspiring the reader's imagination.

Similes are stated comparisons using "like" or "as." Similes can be used to stimulate readers' imaginations and appeal to their senses. Because a simile includes *like* or *as,* the device creates more space between the description and the thing being described than a metaphor does. If an author says that *a house was like a shoebox*, then the tone is different than the author saying that the house *was* a shoebox. Authors will choose between a metaphor and a simile depending on their intended tone.

Similes also help compare fictional characters to well-known objects or experiences, so the reader can better relate to them. William Wordsworth's poem about "Daffodils" begins, "I wandered lonely as a cloud." This simile compares his loneliness to that of a cloud. It is also personification, giving a cloud the human quality loneliness. In his novel *Lord Jim* (1900), Joseph Conrad writes in Chapter 33, "I would have given anything for the power to soothe her frail soul, tormenting itself in its invincible ignorance like a small bird beating about the cruel wires of a cage." Conrad uses the word "like" to compare the girl's soul to a small bird. His description of the bird beating at the cage shows the similar helplessness of the girl's soul to gain freedom.

Ted Hughes frequently used animal metaphors in his poetry. In "The Thought Fox," a model of concise, structured beauty, Hughes characterizes the poet's creative process with succinct, striking imagery of an idea entering his head like a wild fox. Repeating "loneliness" in the first two stanzas emphasizes the poet's lonely work: "Something else is alive / Beside the clock's loneliness." He treats an idea's arrival as separate from himself. Three stanzas detail in vivid images a fox's approach from the outside winter forest at starless midnight—its nose, "Cold, delicately" touching twigs and leaves; "neat" paw prints in snow; "bold" body; brilliant green eyes; and self-contained, focused progress— "Till, with a sudden sharp hot stink of fox," he metaphorically depicts poetic inspiration as the fox's physical entry into "the dark hole of the head." Hughes ends by summarizing his vision of a poet as an interior, passive idea recipient, with the outside world unchanged: "The window is starless still; the clock ticks, / The page is printed."

A **metaphor** is an implied comparison, i.e. it compares something to something else without using "like", "as", or other comparative words. For example, in "The Tyger" (1794), William Blake writes, "Tyger Tyger, burning bright, / In the forests of the night." Blake compares the tiger to a flame not by saying it is like a fire, but by simply describing it as "burning." Henry Wadsworth Longfellow's poem "O Ship of State" (1850) uses an extended metaphor by referring consistently throughout the entire poem to the state, union, or republic as a seagoing vessel, referring to its keel, mast, sail, rope, anchors, and to its braving waves, rocks, gale, tempest, and "false lights on the shore." Within the extended metaphor, Wordsworth uses a specific metaphor: "the anchors of thy hope!"

In literature, irony demonstrates the opposite of what is said or done. The three types of irony are **verbal irony**, **situational irony**, and **dramatic irony**. Verbal irony uses words opposite to the meaning. Sarcasm may use verbal irony. One common example is describing something that is confusing as "clear as mud." For example, in his 1986 movie *Hannah and Her Sisters,* author, director, and actor Woody Allen says to his character's date, "I had a great evening; it was like the Nuremburg Trials." Notice these employ similes. In situational irony, what happens contrasts with what was expected. O. Henry's short story *The Gift of the Magi* uses situational irony: a husband and wife each sacrifice their most prized possession to buy each other a Christmas present. The irony is that she sells her long hair to buy him a watch fob, while he sells his heirloom pocket-watch to buy her the jeweled combs for her hair she had long wanted; in the end, neither of them can use their gifts. In dramatic irony, narrative informs audiences of more than its characters know. For example, in *Romeo and Juliet,* the audience is made aware that Juliet is only asleep, while Romeo believes her to be dead, which then leads to Romeo's death.

Hyperbole is excessive exaggeration used for humor or emphasis rather than for literal meaning. For example, in *To Kill a Mockingbird*, Harper Lee wrote, "People moved slowly then. There was no hurry, for there was nowhere to go, nothing to buy and no money to buy it with, nothing to see outside the boundaries of Maycomb County." This was not literally true; Lee exaggerates the scarcity of these things for emphasis. In "Old Times on the Mississippi," Mark Twain wrote, "I... could have hung my hat on my eyes, they stuck out so far." This is not literal, but makes his description vivid and funny. In his poem "As I Walked Out One Evening", W. H. Auden wrote, "I'll love you, dear, I'll love you / Till China and Africa meet, / And the river jumps over the mountain / And the salmon sing in the street." He used things not literally possible to emphasize the duration of his love.

Reading
© Mometrix Media - flashcardsecrets.com/louisiana
English I

Describe what a simile is.

Reading
© Mometrix Media - flashcardsecrets.com/louisiana
English I

Describe what a metaphor is.

Reading
© Mometrix Media - flashcardsecrets.com/louisiana
English I

Define and give a literary example of metaphor from a poem, explaining how it fits the definition. Name a poem that uses an extended metaphor, identifying the extended metaphor.

Reading
© Mometrix Media - flashcardsecrets.com/louisiana
English I

Explicate how poet Ted Hughes embodies the concept of inspiration to write in an animal metaphor.

Reading
© Mometrix Media - flashcardsecrets.com/louisiana
English I

Define and give several examples of hyperbole as a kind of figurative language used in literature.

Reading
© Mometrix Media - flashcardsecrets.com/louisiana
English I

Define three types of literary irony. Give some examples in literature of two of these types.

When language is used **literally**, the words mean exactly what they say and nothing more. When language is used **figuratively**, the words mean something beyond their literal meaning. For example, "The weeping willow tree has long, trailing branches and leaves" is a literal description. But "The weeping willow tree looks as if it is bending over and crying" is a figurative description—specifically, a **simile** or stated comparison. Another figurative language form is **metaphor**, or an implied comparison. A good example is the metaphor of a city, state, or city-state as a ship, and its governance as sailing that ship. Ancient Greek lyrical poet Alcaeus is credited with first using this metaphor, and ancient Greek tragedian Aeschylus then used it in *Seven Against Thebes,* and then Plato used it in the *Republic*.

A summary of a literary passage is a condensation in the reader's own words of the passage's main points. Several guidelines can be used in evaluating a summary. The summary should be complete yet concise. It should be accurate, balanced, fair, neutral, and objective, excluding the reader's own opinions or reactions. It should reflect in similar proportion how much each point summarized was covered in the original passage. Summary writers should include tags of attribution, like "Macaulay argues that" to reference the original author whose ideas are represented in the summary. Summary writers should not overuse quotations; they should only quote central concepts or phrases they cannot precisely convey in words other than those of the original author. Another aspect of evaluating a summary is considering whether it can stand alone as a coherent, unified composition. In addition, evaluation of a summary should include whether its writer has cited the original source of the passage they have summarized so that readers can find it.

Figurative language extends past the literal meanings of words. It offers readers new insight into the people, things, events, and subjects covered in a work of literature. Figurative language also enables readers to feel they are sharing the authors' experiences. It can stimulate the reader's senses, make comparisons that readers find intriguing or even startling, and enable readers to view the world in different ways. When looking for figurative language, it is important to consider the context of the sentence or situation. Phrases that appear out of place or make little sense when read literally are likely instances of figurative language. Once figurative language has been recognized, context is also important to determining the type of figurative language being used and its function. For example, when a comparison is being made, a metaphor or simile is likely being used. This means the comparison may emphasize or create irony through the things being compared. Seven specific types of figurative language include: alliteration, onomatopoeia, personification, imagery, similes, metaphors, and hyperbole.

A **figure of speech** is a verbal expression whose meaning is figurative rather than literal. For example, the phrase "butterflies in the stomach" does not refer to actual butterflies in a person's stomach. It is a metaphor representing the fluttery feelings experienced when a person is nervous or excited—or when one "falls in love," which does not mean physically falling. "Hitting a sales target" does not mean physically hitting a target with arrows as in archery; it is a metaphor for meeting a sales quota. "Climbing the ladder of success" metaphorically likens advancing in one's career to ascending ladder rungs. Similes, such as "light as a feather" (meaning very light, not a feather's actual weight), and hyperbole, like "I'm starving/freezing/roasting," are also figures of speech. Figures of speech are often used and crafted for emphasis, freshness of expression, or clarity.

Another type of figurative language is **personification**. This is describing a non-human thing, like an animal or an object, as if it were human. The general intent of personification is to describe things in a manner that will be comprehensible to readers. When an author states that a tree *groans* in the wind, he or she does not mean that the tree is emitting a low, pained sound from a mouth. Instead, the author means that the tree is making a noise similar to a human groan. Of course, this personification establishes a tone of sadness or suffering. A different tone would be established if the author said that the tree was *swaying* or *dancing*. Alfred Tennyson's poem "The Eagle" uses all of these types of figurative language: "He clasps the crag with crooked hands." Tennyson used alliteration, repeating /k/ and /kr/ sounds. These hard-sounding consonants reinforce the imagery, giving visual and tactile impressions of the eagle.

Alliteration describes a series of words beginning with the same sounds. **Onomatopoeia** uses words imitating the sounds of things they name or describe. For example, in his poem "Come Down, O Maid," Alfred Tennyson writes of "The moan of doves in immemorial elms, / And murmuring of innumerable bees." The word "moan" sounds like some sounds doves make, "murmuring" represents the sounds of bees buzzing. Onomatopoeia also includes words that are simply meant to represent sounds, such as "meow," "kaboom," and "whoosh."

Reading
© Mometrix Media - flashcardsecrets.com/louisiana
English I

Describe some guidelines for evaluating a summary of a passage from a work of literature.

Reading
© Mometrix Media - flashcardsecrets.com/louisiana
English I

Explain the distinction between literal meaning and figurative meaning in literature, including some examples.

Reading
© Mometrix Media - flashcardsecrets.com/louisiana
English I

Define what figures of speech are and give some examples.

Reading
© Mometrix Media - flashcardsecrets.com/louisiana
English I

Give a general definition of figurative language in literature and identify two functions it serves. Identify seven specific types of figurative language.

Reading
© Mometrix Media - flashcardsecrets.com/louisiana
English I

Define alliteration and onomatopoeia.

Reading
© Mometrix Media - flashcardsecrets.com/louisiana
English I

Describe what personification is.

When presented with two different stories, there will be **similarities** and **differences** between the two. A reader needs to make a list, or other graphic organizer, of the points presented in each story. Once the reader has written down the main point and supporting points for each story, the two sets of ideas can be compared. The reader can then present each idea and show how it is the same or different in the other story. This is called **comparing and contrasting ideas**.

The reader can compare ideas by stating, for example: "In Story 1, the author believes that humankind will one day land on Mars, whereas in Story 2, the author believes that Mars is too far away for humans to ever step foot on." Note that the two viewpoints are different in each story that the reader is comparing. A reader may state that: "Both stories discussed the likelihood of humankind landing on Mars." This statement shows how the viewpoint presented in both stories is based on the same topic, rather than how each viewpoint is different. The reader will complete a comparison of two stories with a conclusion.

Ideas from a text can also be organized using **graphic organizers**. A graphic organizer is a way to simplify information and take key points from the text. A graphic organizer such as a timeline may have an event listed for a corresponding date on the timeline, while an outline may have an event listed under a key point that occurs in the text. Each reader needs to create the type of graphic organizer that works the best for him or her in terms of being able to recall information from a story. Examples include a spider-map, which takes a main idea from the story and places it in a bubble with supporting points branching off the main idea. An outline is useful for diagramming the main and supporting points of the entire story, and a Venn diagram compares and contrasts characteristics of two or more ideas.

It is important to understand the logical conclusion of the ideas presented in an informational text. **Identifying a logical conclusion** can help you determine whether you agree with the writer or not. Coming to this conclusion is much like making an inference: the approach requires you to combine the information given by the text with what you already know and make a logical conclusion. If the author intended for the reader to draw a certain conclusion, then you can expect the author's argumentation and detail to be leading in that direction.

One way to approach the task of drawing conclusions is to make brief **notes** of all the points made by the author. When the notes are arranged on paper, they may clarify the logical conclusion. Another way to approach conclusions is to consider whether the reasoning of the author raises any pertinent questions. Sometimes you will be able to draw several conclusions from a passage. On occasion these will be conclusions that were never imagined by the author. Therefore, be aware that these conclusions must be **supported directly by the text**.

Read the following sentence from *Little Women* by Louisa May Alcott and draw a conclusion based upon the information presented:

> *You know the reason Mother proposed not having any presents this Christmas was because it is going to be a hard winter for everyone; and she thinks we ought not to spend money for pleasure, when our men are suffering so in the army.*

Based on the information in the sentence, the reader can conclude, or **infer**, that the men are away at war while the women are still at home. The pronoun *our* gives a clue to the reader that the character is speaking about men she knows. In addition, the reader can assume that the character is speaking to a brother or sister, since the term "Mother" is used by the character while speaking to another person. The reader can also come to the conclusion that the characters celebrate Christmas, since it is mentioned in the **context** of the sentence. In the sentence, the Mother is presented as an unselfish character who is opinionated and thinks about the wellbeing of other people.

As an aid to drawing conclusions, **outlining** the information contained in the passage should be a familiar skill to readers. An effective outline will reveal the structure of the passage and will lead to solid conclusions. An effective outline will have a title that refers to the basic subject of the text, though the title does not need to restate the main idea. In most outlines, the main idea will be the first major section. Each major idea in the passage will be established as the head of a category. For instance, the most common outline format calls for the main ideas of the passage to be indicated with Roman numerals. In an effective outline of this kind, each of the main ideas will be represented by a Roman numeral and none of the Roman numerals will designate minor details or secondary ideas. Moreover, all supporting ideas and details should be placed in the appropriate place on the outline. An outline does not need to include every detail listed in the text, but it should feature all of those that are central to the argument or message. Each of these details should be listed under the corresponding main idea.

A helpful tool is the ability to **summarize** the information that you have read in a paragraph or passage format. This process is similar to creating an effective outline. First, a summary should accurately define the main idea of the passage, though the summary does not need to explain this main idea in exhaustive detail. The summary should continue by laying out the most important supporting details or arguments from the passage. All of the significant supporting details should be included, and none of the details included should be irrelevant or insignificant. Also, the summary should accurately report all of these details. Too often, the desire for brevity in a summary leads to the sacrifice of clarity or accuracy. Summaries are often difficult to read because they omit all of the graceful language, digressions, and asides that distinguish great writing. However, an effective summary should communicate the same overall message as the original text.

Reading
© Mometrix Media - flashcardsecrets.com/louisiana
English I

Discuss how readers can infer character traits based on dialogue.

Reading
© Mometrix Media - flashcardsecrets.com/louisiana
English I

Describe the process of comparing two stories and identifying similarities and differences between them.

Reading
© Mometrix Media - flashcardsecrets.com/louisiana
English I

Discuss the process of identifying an effective outline of information presented in a paragraph or message.

Reading
© Mometrix Media - flashcardsecrets.com/louisiana
English I

Explain the ways that a reader can use graphic organizers to order the ideas that are presented in a text.

Reading
© Mometrix Media - flashcardsecrets.com/louisiana
English I

Discuss summarizing.

Visit *mometrix.com/academy* for a related video.
Enter video code: 172903

Reading
© Mometrix Media - flashcardsecrets.com/louisiana
English I

Discuss the process of identifying the logical conclusion in a reading selection.

Usually, identifying the author's **purpose** is easier than identifying his or her position. In most cases, the author has no interest in hiding his or her purpose. A text that is meant to entertain, for instance, should be written to please the reader. Most narratives, or stories, are written to entertain, though they may also inform or persuade. Informative texts are easy to identify, while the most difficult purpose of a text to identify is persuasion because the author has an interest in making this purpose hard to detect. When a reader discovers that the author is trying to persuade, he or she should be skeptical of the argument. For this reason, persuasive texts often try to establish an entertaining tone and hope to amuse the reader into agreement. On the other hand, an informative tone may be implemented to create an appearance of authority and objectivity.

In order to be an effective reader, one must pay attention to the author's **position** and **purpose**. Even those texts that seem objective and impartial, like textbooks, have a position and bias. Readers need to take these positions into account when considering the author's message. When an author uses emotional language or clearly favors one side of an argument, his or her position is clear. However, the author's position may be evident not only in what he or she writes, but also in what he or she doesn't write. In a normal setting, a reader would want to review some other texts on the same topic in order to develop a view of the author's position. If this was not possible, then you would want to at least acquire some background about the author. However, since you are in the middle of an exam and the only source of information is the text, you should look for language and argumentation that seems to indicate a particular stance on the subject.

A reader should always be drawing conclusions from the text. Sometimes conclusions are **implied** from written information, and other times the information is **stated directly** within the passage. One should always aim to draw conclusions from information stated within a passage, rather than to draw them from mere implications. At times an author may provide some information and then describe a counterargument. Readers should be alert for direct statements that are subsequently rejected or weakened by the author. Furthermore, you should always read through the entire passage before drawing conclusions. Many readers are trained to expect the author's conclusions at either the beginning or the end of the passage, but many texts do not adhere to this format.

An author's purpose is evident often in the organization of the text (e.g., section headings in bold font points to an informative text). However, you may not have such organization available to you in your exam. Instead, if the author makes his or her main idea clear from the beginning, then the likely purpose of the text is to inform. If the author begins by making a claim and provides various arguments to support that claim, then the purpose is probably to persuade. If the author tells a story or wants to gain the reader's attention more than to push a particular point or deliver information, then his or her purpose is most likely to entertain. As a reader, you must judge authors on how well they accomplish their purpose. In other words, you need to consider the type of passage (e.g., technical, persuasive, etc.) that the author has written and if the author has followed the requirements of the passage type.

A common type of inference that a reader has to make is **drawing a conclusion**. The reader makes this conclusion based on the information provided within a text. Certain facts are included to help a reader come to a specific conclusion. For example, a story may open with a man trudging through the snow on a cold winter day, dragging a sled behind him. The reader can logically **infer** from the setting of the story that the man is wearing heavy winter clothes in order to stay warm. Information is implied based on the setting of a story, which is why **setting** is an important element of the text. If the same man in the example was trudging down a beach on a hot summer day, dragging a surf board behind him, the reader would assume that the man is not wearing heavy clothes. The reader makes inferences based on their own experiences and the information presented to them in the story.

Test-taking tip: When asked to identify a conclusion that may be drawn, look for critical "hedge" phrases, such as *likely*, *may*, *can*, and *will often*, among many others. When you are being tested on this knowledge, remember the question that writers insert into these hedge phrases to cover every possibility. Often an answer will be wrong simply because there is no room for exception. Extreme positive or negative answers (such as always or never) are usually not correct. When answering these questions, the reader **should not** use any outside knowledge that is not gathered directly or reasonably inferred from the passage. Correct answers can be derived straight from the passage.

Drawing conclusions from information implied within a passage requires confidence on the part of the reader. **Implications** are things that the author does not state directly, but readers can assume based on what the author does say. Consider the following passage: *I stepped outside and opened my umbrella. By the time I got to work, the cuffs of my pants were soaked.* The author never states that it is raining, but this fact is clearly implied. Conclusions based on implication must be well supported by the text. In order to draw a solid conclusion, readers should have **multiple pieces of evidence**. If readers have only one piece, they must be assured that there is no other possible explanation than their conclusion. A good reader will be able to draw many conclusions from information implied by the text, which will be a great help on the exam.

Reading
© Mometrix Media - flashcardsecrets.com/louisiana
English I

Discuss strategies for identifying an author's position.

Reading
© Mometrix Media - flashcardsecrets.com/louisiana
English I

Discuss issues related to identifying an author's purpose.

Reading
© Mometrix Media - flashcardsecrets.com/louisiana
English I

Review some strategies for identifying an author's purpose.

Reading
© Mometrix Media - flashcardsecrets.com/louisiana
English I

Discuss the process of drawing conclusions from information stated directly within a passage.

Reading
© Mometrix Media - flashcardsecrets.com/louisiana
English I

Discuss the process of drawing conclusions from information implied within a passage.

Reading
© Mometrix Media - flashcardsecrets.com/louisiana
English I

Explain why drawing a conclusion is an important critical reading skill.

Inferences about literary text are logical conclusions that readers make based on their observations and previous knowledge. An inference is based on both what is found in a passage or a story and what is known from personal experience. For instance, a story may say that a character is frightened and can hear howling in the distance. Based on both what is in the text and personal knowledge, it is a logical conclusion that the character is frightened because he hears the sound of wolves. A good inference is supported by the information in a passage.

By inferring, readers construct meanings from text that are personally relevant. By combining their own schemas or concepts and their background information pertinent to the text with what they read, readers interpret it according to both what the author has conveyed and their own unique perspectives. Inferences are different from **explicit information**, which is clearly stated in a passage. Authors do not always explicitly spell out every meaning in what they write; many meanings are implicit. Through inference, readers can comprehend implied meanings in the text, and also derive personal significance from it, making the text meaningful and memorable to them. Inference is a natural process in everyday life. When readers infer, they can draw conclusions about what the author is saying, predict what may reasonably follow, amend these predictions as they continue to read, interpret the import of themes, and analyze the characters' feelings and motivations through their actions.

When making predictions, readers should be able to explain how they developed their prediction. One way readers can defend their thought process is by citing textual evidence. Textual evidence to evaluate reader predictions about literature includes specific synopses of the work, paraphrases of the work or parts of it, and direct quotations from the work. These references to the text must support the prediction by indicating, clearly or unclearly, what will happen later in the story. A text may provide these indications through literary devices such as foreshadowing. Foreshadowing is anything in a text that gives the reader a hint about what is to come by emphasizing the likelihood of an event or development. Foreshadowing can occur through descriptions, exposition, and dialogue. Foreshadowing in dialogue usually occurs when a character gives a warning or expresses a strong feeling that a certain event will occur. Foreshadowing can also occur through irony. However, unlike other forms of foreshadowing, the events that seem the most likely are the opposite of what actually happens. Instances of foreshadowing and irony can be summarized, paraphrased, or quoted to defend a reader's prediction.

Reading involves thinking. For good comprehension, readers make **text-to-self**, **text-to-text**, and **text-to-world connections**. Making connections helps readers understand text better and predict what might occur next based on what they already know, such as how characters in the story feel or what happened in another text. Text-to-self connections with the reader's life and experiences make literature more personally relevant and meaningful to readers. Readers can make connections before, during, and after reading—including whenever the text reminds them of something similar they have encountered in life or other texts. The genre, setting, characters, plot elements, literary structure and devices, and themes an author uses allow a reader to make connections to other works of literature or to people and events in their own lives. Venn diagrams and other graphic organizers help visualize connections. Readers can also make double-entry notes: key content, ideas, events, words, and quotations on one side, and the connections with these on the other.

Read the excerpt and decide why Jana finally relaxed.

Jana loved her job, but the work was very demanding. She had trouble relaxing. She called a friend, but she still thought about work. She ordered a pizza, but eating it did not help. Then, her kitten jumped on her lap and began to purr. Jana leaned back and began to hum a little tune. She felt better.

You can draw the conclusion that Jana relaxed because her kitten jumped on her lap. The kitten purred, and Jana leaned back and hummed a tune. Then she felt better. The excerpt does not explicitly say that this is the reason why she was able to relax. The text leaves the matter unclear, but the reader can infer or make a "best guess" that this is the reason she is relaxing. This is a logical conclusion based on the information in the passage. It is the best conclusion a reader can make based on the information he or she has read. Inferences are based on the information in a passage, but they are not directly stated in the passage.

Test-taking tip: While being tested on your ability to make correct inferences, you must look for **contextual clues**. An answer can be true, but not the best or most correct answer. The contextual clues will help you find the answer that is the **best answer** out of the given choices. Be careful in your reading to understand the context in which a phrase is stated. When asked for the implied meaning of a statement made in the passage, you should immediately locate the statement and read the **context** in which the statement was made. Also, look for an answer choice that has a similar phrase to the statement in question.

Paraphrasing is another method that the reader can use to aid in comprehension. When paraphrasing, one puts what they have read into their own words by rephrasing what the author has written, or one "translates" all of what the author shared into their own words by including as many details as they can.

When reading literature, especially demanding works, **summarizing** helps readers identify important information and organize it in their minds. They can also identify themes, problems, and solutions, and can sequence the story. Readers can summarize before, during, and after they read. They should use their own words, as they do when describing a personal event or giving directions. Previewing a text's organization before reading by examining the book cover, table of contents, and illustrations also aids summarizing. Making notes of key words and ideas in a graphic organizer while reading can benefit readers in the same way. Graphic organizers are another useful method; readers skim the text to determine main ideas and then narrow the list with the aid of the organizer. Unimportant details should be omitted in summaries. Summaries can be organized using description, problem-solution, comparison-contrast, sequence, main ideas, or cause-and-effect.

Reading
© Mometrix Media - flashcardsecrets.com/louisiana
English I

Discuss how textual evidence can be used to support predictions.

Reading
© Mometrix Media - flashcardsecrets.com/louisiana
English I

Define inferences. Explain generally the process of how readers draw inferences from a literary text and discuss how inferences can impact the reader's experience with the text.

Reading
© Mometrix Media - flashcardsecrets.com/louisiana
English I

Draw a conclusion based on an excerpt and defend the conclusion in regard to logic.

Reading
© Mometrix Media - flashcardsecrets.com/louisiana
English I

Explain why, when, and how readers can make connections, and what kinds of connections, to enhance reading comprehension when reading literature.

Reading
© Mometrix Media - flashcardsecrets.com/louisiana
English I

Discuss why, when, and how readers can summarize literature to support their reading comprehension.

Reading
© Mometrix Media - flashcardsecrets.com/louisiana
English I

Discuss paraphrasing.

Many texts follow the **compare-and-contrast** model in which the similarities and differences between two ideas or things are explored. Analysis of the similarities between ideas is called **comparison**. In an ideal comparison, the author places ideas or things in an equivalent structure, i.e., the author presents the ideas in the same way. If an author wants to show the similarities between cricket and baseball, then he or she may do so by summarizing the equipment and rules for each game. Be mindful of the similarities as they appear in the passage and take note of any differences that are mentioned. Often, these small differences will only reinforce the more general similarity.

Some nonfiction texts are organized to **present a problem** followed by a solution. For this type of text, the problem is often explained before the solution is offered. In some cases, as when the problem is well known, the solution may be introduced briefly at the beginning. Other passages may focus on the solution, and the problem will be referenced only occasionally. Some texts will outline multiple solutions to a problem, leaving readers to choose among them. If the author has an interest or an allegiance to one solution, he or she may fail to mention or describe accurately some of the other solutions. Readers should be careful of the author's agenda when reading a problem-solution text. Only by understanding the author's perspective and interests can one develop a proper judgment of the proposed solution.

Readers must be able to identify a text's **sequence**, or the order in which things happen. Often, when the sequence is very important to the author, the text is indicated with signal words like *first*, *then*, *next*, and *last*. However, a sequence can be merely implied and must be noted by the reader. Consider the sentence *He walked through the garden and gave water and fertilizer to the plants*. Clearly, the man did not walk through the garden before he collected water and fertilizer for the plants. So, the implied sequence is that he first collected water, then he collected fertilizer, next he walked through the garden, and last he gave water or fertilizer as necessary to the plants. Texts do not always proceed in an orderly sequence from first to last. Sometimes they begin at the end and start over at the beginning. As a reader, you can enhance your understanding of the passage by taking brief notes to clarify the sequence.

Thinking critically about ideas and conclusions can seem like a daunting task. One way to ease this task is to understand the basic elements of ideas and writing techniques. Looking at the ways different ideas relate to each other can be a good way for readers to begin their analysis. For instance, sometimes authors will write about two ideas that are in opposition to each other. Or, one author will provide his or her ideas on a topic, and another author may respond in opposition. The analysis of these opposing ideas is known as **contrast**. Contrast is often marred by the author's obvious partiality to one of the ideas. A discerning reader will be put off by an author who does not engage in a fair fight. In an analysis of opposing ideas, both ideas should be presented in clear and reasonable terms. If the author does prefer a side, you need to read carefully to determine the areas where the author shows or avoids this preference. In an analysis of opposing ideas, you should proceed through the passage by marking the major differences point by point with an eye that is looking for an explanation of each side's view. For instance, in an analysis of capitalism and communism, there is an importance in outlining each side's view on labor, markets, prices, personal responsibility, etc. Additionally, as you read through the passages, you should note whether the opposing views present each side in a similar manner.

As we read on, we can test the accuracy of our predictions, revise them in light of additional reading, and confirm or refute our predictions. Predictions are always subject to revision as the reader acquires more information. A reader can make predictions by observing the title and illustrations; noting the structure, characters, and subject; drawing on existing knowledge relative to the subject; and asking "why" and "who" questions. Connecting reading to what we already know enables us to learn new information and construct meaning. For example, before third-graders read a book about Johnny Appleseed, they may start a KWL chart—a list of what they *Know*, what they *Want* to know or learn, and what they have *Learned* after reading. Activating existing background knowledge and thinking about the text before reading improves comprehension.

Test-taking tip: To respond to questions requiring future predictions, your answers should be based on evidence of past or present behavior and events.

When we read literature, **making predictions** about what will happen in the writing reinforces our purpose for reading and prepares us mentally. A **prediction** is a guess about what will happen next. Readers constantly make predictions based on what they have read and what they already know. We can make predictions before we begin reading and during our reading. Consider the following sentence: *Staring at the computer screen in shock, Kim blindly reached over for the brimming glass of water on the shelf to her side*. The sentence suggests that Kim is distracted, and that she is not looking at the glass that she is going to pick up. So, a reader might predict that Kim is going to knock over the glass. Of course, not every prediction will be accurate: perhaps Kim will pick the glass up cleanly. Nevertheless, the author has certainly created the expectation that the water might be spilled.

Reading
© Mometrix Media - flashcardsecrets.com/louisiana
English I

Describe the problem-solution text structure.

Reading
© Mometrix Media - flashcardsecrets.com/louisiana
English I

Describe the compare-and-contrast structure.

Reading
© Mometrix Media - flashcardsecrets.com/louisiana
English I

Describe how contrast can be used as a critical thinking tool.

Reading
© Mometrix Media - flashcardsecrets.com/louisiana
English I

Describe how a sequence is presented in writing.

Visit *mometrix.com/academy* for a related video.
Enter video code: 489027

Reading
© Mometrix Media - flashcardsecrets.com/louisiana
English I

Discuss some aspects of making predictions as a literacy skill to support reading comprehension.

Reading
© Mometrix Media - flashcardsecrets.com/louisiana
English I

Discuss some aspects of making predictions as a literacy skill to support reading comprehension.

The way a text is organized can help readers understand the author's intent and his or her conclusions. There are various ways to organize a text, and each one has a purpose and use. Usually, authors will organize information logically in a passage so the reader can follow and locate the information within the text. However, since not all passages are written with the same logical structure, you need to be familiar with several different types of passage structure.

Supporting details are smaller pieces of evidence that provide backing for the main point. In order to show that a main idea is correct or valid, an author must add details that prove their point. All texts contain details, but they are only classified as supporting details when they serve to reinforce some larger point. Supporting details are most commonly found in informative and persuasive texts. In some cases, they will be clearly indicated with terms like *for example* or *for instance*, or they will be enumerated with terms like *first*, *second*, and *last*. However, you need to be prepared for texts that do not contain those indicators. As a reader, you should consider whether the author's supporting details really back up his or her main point. Details can be factual and correct, yet they may not be **relevant** to the author's point. Conversely, details can be relevant, but be ineffective because they are based on opinion or assertions that cannot be proven.

An example of a main idea is: *Giraffes live in the Serengeti of Africa*. A supporting detail about giraffes could be: *A giraffe in this region benefits from a long neck by reaching twigs and leaves on tall trees*. The main idea gives the general idea that the text is about giraffes. The supporting detail gives a specific fact about how the giraffes eat.

One of the most common text structures is **cause and effect**. A **cause** is an act or event that makes something happen, and an **effect** is the thing that happens as a result of the cause. A cause-and-effect relationship is not always explicit, but there are some terms in English that signal causes, such as *since*, *because*, and *due to*. Furthermore, terms that signal effects include *consequently, therefore, this leads to*. As an example, consider the sentence *Because the sky was clear, Ron did not bring an umbrella*. The cause is the clear sky, and the effect is that Ron did not bring an umbrella. However, readers may find that sometimes the cause-and-effect relationship will not be clearly noted. For instance, the sentence *He was late and missed the meeting* does not contain any signaling words, but the sentence still contains a cause (he was late) and an effect (he missed the meeting).

When using **chronological** order, the author presents information in the order that it happened. For example, biographies are typically written in chronological order. The subject's birth and childhood are presented first, followed by their adult life, and lastly the events leading up to the person's death.

Persuasive essays, in which an author tries to make a convincing argument and change the minds of readers, usually include cause-and-effect relationships. However, these relationships should not always be taken at face value. Frequently, an author will assume a cause or take an effect for granted. To read a persuasive essay effectively, readers need to judge the cause-and-effect relationships that the author is presenting. For instance, imagine an author wrote the following: *The parking deck has been unprofitable because people would prefer to ride their bikes*. The relationship is clear: the cause is that people prefer to ride their bikes, and the effect is that the parking deck has been unprofitable. However, readers should consider whether this argument is conclusive. Perhaps there are other reasons for the failure of the parking deck: a down economy, excessive fees, etc. Too often, authors present causal relationships as if they are fact rather than opinion. Readers should be on the alert for these dubious claims.

Be aware of the possibility for a single cause to have **multiple effects.** (e.g., *Single cause*: Because you left your homework on the table, your dog engulfed the assignment. *Multiple effects*: As a result, you receive a failing grade, your parents do not allow you to go out with your friends, you miss out on the new movie, and one of your classmates spoils it for you before you have another chance to watch it).

Also, there is the possibility for a single effect to have **multiple causes.** (e.g., *Single effect*: Alan has a fever. *Multiple causes*: An unexpected cold front came through the area, and Alan forgot to take his multi-vitamin to avoid getting sick.) Additionally, an effect can in turn be the cause of another effect, in what is known as a cause-and-effect chain. (e.g., As a result of her disdain for procrastination, Lynn prepared for her exam. This led to her passing her test with high marks. Hence, her resume was accepted and her application was approved.)

Reading
© Mometrix Media - flashcardsecrets.com/louisiana
English I

Discuss the identification and evaluation of supporting details.

Reading
© Mometrix Media - flashcardsecrets.com/louisiana
English I

Discuss why organizational structures vary as well as why readers need to be familiar with different types.

Reading
© Mometrix Media - flashcardsecrets.com/louisiana
English I

Describe the use of chronological order as an organizational structure.

Reading
© Mometrix Media - flashcardsecrets.com/louisiana
English I

Describe how an author demonstrates cause and effect.

Visit *mometrix.com/academy* for a related video.
Enter video code: 725944

Reading
© Mometrix Media - flashcardsecrets.com/louisiana
English I

Explain how a single cause can have multiple effects, how a single effect can have multiple causes, and the cause-and-effect chain.

Reading
© Mometrix Media - flashcardsecrets.com/louisiana
English I

Describe persuasive essays, including some common pitfalls of persuasive writing.

Literary authors often use dialect when writing dialogue to illustrate the social and geographical backgrounds of specific characters, which supports character development. For example, in *The Adventures of Huckleberry Finn* (1885), Mark Twain's novel is written in the dialect of a young, uneducated, white, Southern character, opening with this sentence: "You don't know about me without you have read a book by the name of The Adventures of Tom Sawyer, but that ain' no matter." Twain uses a different and exaggerated dialect to represent the speech of the African-American slave Jim: "We's safe, Huck, we's safe! Jump up and crack yo' heels. Dat's de good ole Cairo at las', I jis know it."

In *To Kill a Mockingbird,* author Harper Lee used dialect in the characters' dialogue to portray an uneducated boy in the American South: "Reckon I have. Almost died the first year I come to school and et them pecans—folks say he pizened 'em." Lee also uses many Southern regional expressions, such as "right stove up," "What in the sam holy hill?", "sit a spell," "fess" (meaning "confess"), "jim-dandy," and "hush your fussing." These contribute to Lee's characterization of the people she describes, who live in a small town in Alabama circa the 1930s. In *Wuthering Heights* (1847), Emily Bronte reproduces Britain's 18th–19th-century Yorkshire dialect in the speech of servant Joseph: "Running after t'lads, as usuald!... If I war yah, maister, I'd just slam t'boards i' their faces all on 'em, gentle and simple! Never a day ut yah're off, but yon cat o' Linton comes sneaking hither; and Miss Nelly, shoo's a fine lass!"

Linguistic researchers have identified regional variations in vocabulary choices, which have evolved because of differences in local climates and how they influence human behaviors. For example, in the Southern United States, the Linguistic Atlas of the Gulf States (LAGS) Project by Dr. Lee Pederson of Emory University discovered and documented that people living in the northern or Upland section of the Piedmont plateau region call the fungal infection commonly known as athlete's foot "toe itch," but people living in the southern or Lowland section call it "ground itch." The explanation for this difference is that in the north, temperatures are cooler and people wear shoes accordingly, so they associate the itching with the feet in their description, but in the south, temperatures are hotter and people often went barefoot, so they associated the itching with the ground that presumably transmitted the infection.

One of the most important skills in reading comprehension is the identification of **topics** and **main ideas**. There is a subtle difference between these two features. The topic is the subject of a text (i.e., what the text is all about). The main idea, on the other hand, is the most important point being made by the author. The topic is usually expressed in a few words at the most while the main idea often needs a full sentence to be completely defined. As an example, a short passage might be written on the topic of penguins, and the main idea could be written as *Penguins are different from other birds in many ways*. In most nonfiction writing, the topic and the main idea will be **stated directly** and often appear in a sentence at the very beginning or end of the text. When being tested on an understanding of the author's topic, you may be able to skim the passage for the general idea by reading only the first sentence of each paragraph. A body paragraph's first sentence is often—but not always—the main **topic sentence** which gives you a summary of the content in the paragraph.

However, there are cases in which the reader must figure out an **unstated** topic or main idea. In these instances, you must read every sentence of the text and try to come up with an overarching idea that is supported by each of those sentences.

Note: The main idea should not be confused with the thesis statement. While the main idea gives a brief, general summary of a text, the thesis statement provides a **specific perspective** on an issue that the author supports with evidence.

Dialects are formed primarily through the influences of location and time, but can be the result of other elements of **social stratification** as well (economic, ethnic, religious, etc.). As one group of a language's speakers is separated from another, in British and American English speakers for example, the language develops in isolated locations at the same time, resulting in distinct dialects. Language changes continuously over time as new words and phrases are adopted and others are phased out. Eventually, these small changes result culminate into enough grammar and vocabulary changes that the speakers of the distinct dialects cannot easily communicate with one another. The dialects can then be recognized as distinct languages.

When written as characters' dialogue in literary works, dialect represents the particular pronunciation, grammar, and figurative expressions used by certain groups of people based on their geographic region, social class, and cultural background. For example, when a character says, "There's gold up in them thar hills," the author is using dialect to add to the characterization of that individual. Diction is more related to individual characters than to groups of people. The way in which a specific character speaks, including his or her choice of words, manner of expressing himself or herself, and use of grammar all represent individual types of diction. For example, two characters in the same novel might describe the same action or event using different diction: One says "I'm heading uptown for the evening," and the other says "I'm going out for a night on the town." These convey the same literal meaning, but due to their variations in diction, the speakers are expressing themselves in slightly different ways.

Dialect is most appropriate for informal or creative writing. Using dialectal writing when communicating casually or informally, such as in a text message or a quick email to a peer, is acceptable. However, in academic and professional contexts, writing using indications of dialect is inappropriate and often unacceptable. If the audience includes individuals who have a higher rank than the author, or authority over the author, it is best not to write in a way that suggests a dialect.

Reading
© Mometrix Media - flashcardsecrets.com/louisiana
English I

Define dialect and discuss how dialects develop over time.

Reading
© Mometrix Media - flashcardsecrets.com/louisiana
English I

Define dialect, giving a reason it is used in literature and some examples.

Reading
© Mometrix Media - flashcardsecrets.com/louisiana
English I

Differentiate between dialect and diction as they are used in literary dialogue, including examples.

Reading
© Mometrix Media - flashcardsecrets.com/louisiana
English I

Comment on some examples of how regional dialect is influenced by such factors as local weather and customs.

Reading
© Mometrix Media - flashcardsecrets.com/louisiana
English I

Discuss the proper use of dialect in writing.

Reading
© Mometrix Media - flashcardsecrets.com/louisiana
English I

Compare and contrast topics and main ideas.

Postcolonial theory involves the historical and geographical context of a work and leads readers to consider how colonization informs the plot, characters, setting, and other elements in the work.

Gender and feminist theory invites readers to interpret a text by looking at its treatment of and suggestions about women and a culture's treatment of women. As with most literary theories, this information can be clearly stated or strongly implied in a work, but it may also be gleaned through looking closely at symbols, characters, and plot elements in a work.

Structuralism uses the structure and organization of a work and the foundations of language to examine how and what a text conveys about the human experience and how those findings connect to common human experiences.

New historicism heavily relies on the cultural and historical context of a work, including when it was written, where the author lives or lived, the culture and history of that location, and other works from the same culture. New historical readings seek to examine these details to expose the ideologies of the location and culture that influenced the work.

Reader-response theory uses the individual reader's response to the text and experience while reading the text to examine the meaning of the reader's relationship with the text and what that relationship suggests about the reader or the factors impacting their experience.

Sociological criticism considers the societies that are relevant to a text. The author's society and any reader's society are important to the text, as sociological criticism seeks to uncover what the text implies or reveals about those societies. This method of criticism can also involve studying the presentation of a society within the text and applying it to the author's society or their other writings.

Literary theory includes ideas that guide readers through the process of interpreting literature. Literary theory, as a subject, encompasses several specific, focused theories that lead readers to interpret or analyze literature through the context of the theory using the subjects and elements it involves. Some commonly used and discussed literary theories include **postcolonial theory**, **gender and feminist theory**, **structuralism**, **new historicism**, **reader-response theory**, and **sociological criticism**.

While dialect and diction are heavily influenced by an individual's culture and the location and history of the place they live, other personal factors can also impact language. A person's ethnicity, religious beliefs or background, and gender can influence the way they use and understand language. **Ethnicity** impacts language by incorporating a group's communication norms into an individual's speech and behavior. These norms may affect a speaker's tone, volume, or pace. These factors may lead others outside of that group to misinterpret the speaker's message, depending on their understanding of how those factors are used in speech. A person's **religious beliefs** can also affect their use of language. Religious beliefs and practices may lead an individual to abstain from using certain terms and may change the context in which a speaker uses specific words, or change their understanding of the word's usage. Additionally a person may use language differently depending on their gender. **Gender's** influence on communication varies by region and industry. A region or industry's treatment of gender roles often impacts language use among its members. This can lead members of one gender group to be more assertive or submissive or to use different terms and phrases.

Language is a diverse tool that allows people to communicate. However, language is often impacted and molded by the culture that uses it. This can make it difficult to learn and use a new language, since not all native speakers of the language will use it or interpret it the same way. For example, English is spoken all over America, but Americans in various regions of the country speak using different **dialects**. Other differences in speech include **accents** and **rhythm of speech**. Language is also manipulated by situations. Some terms and phrases have multiple meanings. A word's meaning often depends on the **context** in which the word or phrase is used, meaning that non-native speakers must learn to interpret situations to understand messages.

Languages are distinct and structured forms of verbal communication. Languages have cohesive sets of rules and words that are shared between the majority of that language's users. The main identifier of a language is that members of one language group are incapable of communicating fluently with members of another language group. New languages are formed as different dialects grow further apart until the members of each dialect can no longer innately communicate with each other.

Dialects are subsets of languages that do not violate the rules of the language as a whole, but which vary from other dialects in vocabulary usage, grammar forms, pronunciation, and spelling. Two major groupings of dialects are American and British English. Most American English and British English speakers can communicate with relative ease with one another, though the pronunciation, vocabulary (torch vs. flashlight; trunk vs. boot), spelling (meter vs. metre; color vs. colour), and grammar (in American English, collective nouns are always considered singular, but can be singular or plural in British English).

Individuals from different countries and cultures communicate differently. Not only do many people speak different languages, but they also speak using different inflections, volumes, tones, and dialects. These factors can have a significant impact on communication, even if the communicators speak the same language. In different cultures, certain behaviors are associated with different meanings and implications. When communicators from different cultures have a conversation, these expectations and associations may lead to misunderstanding. For example, Americans are considered to be louder and more demonstrative than people from other countries. Someone from a country where people speak more quietly who is not aware of this characterization may perceive an American's volume or large gestures as an indication of anger, when in reality, the American speaker is calm. The American may similarly perceive the other person as sad or shy due to their quiet voice, when the speaker is actually happy and comfortable in the conversation. Awareness of these factors and effects promotes respect for others and helps speakers understand the reasons for differences in communication, rather than allowing these differences to create division or conflict.

Reading
© Mometrix Media - flashcardsecrets.com/louisiana
English I

Define literary theory and list specific literary theories.

Reading
© Mometrix Media - flashcardsecrets.com/louisiana
English I

Define postcolonial theory, gender and feminist theory, structuralism, new historicism, reader-response theory, and sociological criticism.

Reading
© Mometrix Media - flashcardsecrets.com/louisiana
English I

Describe ways that culture can affect how an individual communicates.

Reading
© Mometrix Media - flashcardsecrets.com/louisiana
English I

Discuss how ethnicity, religion, and gender can impact a person's understanding and use of a language.

Reading
© Mometrix Media - flashcardsecrets.com/louisiana
English I

Discuss common ways that communication styles differ between different countries.

Reading
© Mometrix Media - flashcardsecrets.com/louisiana
English I

Define language and dialect.

A popular theme throughout literature is the human trait of **reaching too far** or **presuming too much**. In Greek mythology, Daedalus constructed wings of feathers and wax that men might fly like birds. He permitted his son Icarus to try them, but cautioned the boy not to fly too close to the sun. The impetuous youth (in what psychologist David Elkind later named adolescence's myth of invincibility) ignored this, flying too close to the sun. The wax melted, the wings disintegrated, and Icarus fell into the sea and perished. In the Old Testament, God warned Adam and Eve not to eat fruit from the tree of knowledge of good and evil. Because they ignored this command, they were banished from Eden's eternal perfection, condemning them to mortality and suffering. The Romans were themselves examples of overreaching in their conquest and assimilation of most of the then-known world and their ultimate demise. In Christopher Marlowe's *Dr. Faustus* and Johann Wolfgang von Goethe's *Faust,* the protagonist sells his soul to the Devil for unlimited knowledge and success, ultimately leading to his own tragic end.

The Old Testament book of Genesis, the Quran, and the Epic of Gilgamesh all contain flood stories. Versions differ somewhat, yet marketed similarities also exist. Genesis describes a worldwide flood, attributing it to God's decision that mankind, his creation, had become incontrovertibly wicked in spirit and must be destroyed for the world to start anew. The Quran describes the flood as regional, caused by Allah after sending Nuh (notice the similarity in name to Noah) as a messenger to his people to cease their evil. The Quran stipulates that Allah only destroys those who deny or ignore messages from his messengers. In the Gilgamesh poems Utnapishtim, like Noah, is instructed to build a ship to survive the flood. Both men also send out birds afterward as tests, using doves and a raven, though with different outcomes. Many historians and archeologists believe a Middle Eastern tidal wave was a real basis for these stories. However, their universal themes remain the same: the flood was seen as God's way of wiping out humans whose behavior had become ungodly.

Novelist E. M. Forster has made the distinction between story as relating a series of events, such as a king dying and then his queen dying, versus plot as establishing motivations for actions and causes for events, such as a king dying and then his queen dying from grief over his death. Thus, plot fulfills the function of helping readers understand cause-and-effect in events and underlying motivations in characters' actions, which in turn helps them understand life. This affects a work's meaning by supporting its ability to explain why things happen, why people do things, and ultimately the meaning of life. Some authors find that while story events convey meaning, they do not tell readers there is any one meaning in life or way of living, but rather are mental experiments with various meanings, enabling readers to explore. Hence stories may not necessarily be constructed to impose one definitive meaning, but rather to find some shape, direction, and meaning within otherwise random events.

In terms of plot, "story" is the characters, places, and events originating in the author's mind, while "discourse" is how the author arranges and sequences events—which may be chronological or not. Story is imaginary; discourse is words on the page. Discourse allows a story to be told in different ways. One element of plot structure is relating events differently from the order in which they occurred. This is easily done with cause-and-effect; for example, in the sentence, "He died following a long illness," we know the illness preceded the death, but the death precedes the illness in words. In Kate Chopin's short story "The Story of an Hour" (1894), she tells some of the events out of chronological order, which has the effect of amplifying the surprise of the ending for the reader. Another element of plot structure is selection. Chopin omits some details, such as Mr. Mallard's trip home; this allows readers to be as surprised at his arrival as Mrs. Mallard is.

Authors of fiction select characters, places, and events from their imaginations and arrange them to create a story that will affect their readers. One way to analyze plot structure is to compare and contrast different events in a story. For example, in Kate Chopin's "The Story of an Hour," a very simple but key pattern of repetition is the husband's leaving and then returning. Such patterns fulfill the symmetrical aspect that Aristotle said was required of sound plot structure. In James Baldwin's short story, "Sonny's Blues," the narrator is Sonny's brother. In an encounter with one of Sonny's old friends early in the story, the brother initially disregards his communication. In a subsequent flashback, Baldwin informs us that this was the same way he had treated Sonny. In Nathaniel Hawthorne's "Young Goodman Brown," a pattern is created by the protagonist's recurrent efforts not to go farther into the wood. In Herman Melville's "Bartleby the Scrivener" and in William Faulkner's "Barn Burning," patterns are also created by repetition such as Bartleby's repeated refusals and the history of barn-burning episodes, respectively.

In *Poetics,* Aristotle defined plot as "the arrangement of the incidents." He meant not the story, but how it is structured for presentation. In tragedies, Aristotle found results driven by chains of cause and effect preferable to those driven by the protagonist's personality or character. He identified "unity of action" as necessary for a plot's wholeness, meaning its events must be internally connected, not episodic or relying on *deus ex machina* or other external intervention. A plot must have a beginning, middle, and end. Gustav Freytag adapted Aristotle's ideas into his Pyramid (1863). The beginning, today called the exposition, incentive, or inciting moment, emphasizes causes and de-emphasizes effects. Aristotle called the ensuing cause and effect *desis*, or tying up, today called complications which occur during the rising action. These culminate in a crisis or climax, Aristotle's *peripateia*. This occurs at the plot's middle, where cause and effect are both emphasized. The falling action, which Aristotle called the *lusis* or unraveling, is today called the dénouement. The resolution comes at the catastrophe, outcome, or end, when causes are emphasized and effects de-emphasized.

Reading
© Mometrix Media - flashcardsecrets.com/louisiana
English I

Give an example of a topic common to many ancient religious texts, and explain how it reflects a universal theme.

Reading
© Mometrix Media - flashcardsecrets.com/louisiana
English I

Give some examples of the theme of overreaching, in literature and real life, including Greek mythology, the Old Testament, the Romans, and stories of Faust.

Reading
© Mometrix Media - flashcardsecrets.com/louisiana
English I

Differentially define story versus discourse relative to literary plot structure. Define and explain how selection in discourse affects the story using an example.

Reading
© Mometrix Media - flashcardsecrets.com/louisiana
English I

Discuss some ways in which story events in fictional literary narratives affect the works' meanings.

Reading
© Mometrix Media - flashcardsecrets.com/louisiana
English I

Summarize the classic analysis of plot structure as articulated by Aristotle and diagrammed by Gustav Freytag.

Reading
© Mometrix Media - flashcardsecrets.com/louisiana
English I

Use some examples to illustrate how plot structures can be analyzed through recurring patterns in actions or events.

In Victor Hugo's novel *Les Misérables*, the overall metamorphosis of protagonist Jean Valjean from a cynical ex-convict into a noble benefactor demonstrates Hugo's theme of the importance of love and compassion for others. Hugo also reflects this in more specific plot events. For example, Valjean's love for Cosette sustains him through many difficult periods and trying events. Hugo illustrates how love and compassion for others beget the same in them: Bishop Myriel's kindness to Valjean eventually inspires him to become honest. Years later, Valjean, as M. Madeleine, has rescued Fauchelevent from under a fallen carriage, Fauchelevent returns the compassionate act by giving Valjean sanctuary in the convent. M. Myriel's kindness also ultimately enables Valjean to rescue Cosette from the Thénardiers. Receiving Valjean's father-like love enables Cosette to fall in love with and marry Marius, and the love between Cosette and Marius enables the couple to forgive Valjean for his past crimes when they are revealed.

In *The Great Gatsby*, F. Scott Fitzgerald portrayed 1920s America as greedy, cynical, and rife with moral decay. Jay Gatsby's lavish weekly parties symbolize the reckless excesses of the Jazz Age. The growth of bootlegging and organized crime in reaction to Prohibition is symbolized by the character of Meyer Wolfsheim and by Gatsby's own ill-gotten wealth. Fitzgerald symbolized social divisions using geography. The "old money" aristocrats like the Buchanans lived on East Egg, while the "new money" bourgeois like Gatsby lived on West Egg. Fitzgerald also used weather, as many authors have, to reinforce narrative and emotional tones in the novel. Just as in *Romeo and Juliet*, where William Shakespeare set the confrontation of Tybalt and Mercutio and its deadly consequences on the hottest summer day under a burning sun, in *The Great Gatsby*, Fitzgerald did the same with Tom Wilson's deadly confrontation with Gatsby. Both works are ostensible love stories carrying socially critical themes about the destructiveness of pointless and misguided behaviors—family feuds in the former, pursuit of money in the latter.

William Faulkner contrasts the traditions of the antebellum South with the rapid changes of post-Civil War industrialization in his short story "A Rose for Emily." Living inside the isolated world of her house, Emily Grierson denies the reality of modern progress. Contradictorily, she is both a testament to time-honored history and a mysterious, eccentric, unfathomable burden. Faulkner portrays her with deathlike imagery even in life, comparing her to a drowned woman and referring to her skeleton. Emily symbolizes the Old South; as her social status is degraded, so is the antebellum social order. Like Miss Havisham in Charles Dickens' *Great Expectations,* Emily preserves her bridal bedroom, denying change and time's passage. Emily tries to control death through denial, shown in her necrophilia with her father's corpse and her killing of Homer Barron to stop him from leaving her, then also denying his death. Faulkner uses the motif of dust throughout to represent not only the decay of Emily, her house, and Old Southern traditions, but also how her secrets are obscured from others.

In one of his shortest stories, "The Tell-Tale Heart," Poe used economy of language to emphasize the murderer-narrator's obsessive focus on bare details like the victim's cataract-milky eye, the sound of a heartbeat, and insistence he is sane. The narrator begins by denying he is crazy, even citing his extreme agitation as proof of sanity. Contradiction is then extended: the narrator loves the old man, yet kills him. His motives are irrational—not greed or revenge, but to relieve the victim of his "evil eye." Because "eye" and "I" are homonyms, readers may infer that eye/I symbolizes the old man's identity, contradicting the killer's delusion that he can separate them. The narrator distances himself from the old man by perceiving his eye as separate, and dismembering his dead body. This backfires when he imagines the victim's heartbeat, which is really his own, just before he kills him and frequently afterward. Guilty and paranoid, he gives himself away. Poe predated Freud in exploring the paradox of killing those we love and the concept of projecting our own processes onto others.

Because of the old fisherman Santiago's struggle to capture a giant marlin, some people characterize Ernest Hemingway's *The Old Man and the Sea* as telling of man against nature. However, it can more properly be interpreted as telling of man's role as part of nature. Both man and fish are portrayed as brave, proud, and honorable. In Hemingway's world, all creatures, including humans, must either kill or be killed. Santiago reflects, "man can be destroyed but not defeated," following this principle in his life. As heroes are often created through their own deaths, Hemingway seems to believe that while being destroyed is inevitable, destruction enables living beings to transcend it by fighting bravely with honor and dignity. Hemingway echoes Romantic poet John Keats' contention that only immediately before death can we understand beauty as it is about to be destroyed. He also echoes ancient Greek and Roman myths and the Old Testament with the tragic flaw of overweening pride or overreaching. Like Icarus, Prometheus, and Adam and Eve, the old man "went out too far."

The great White Whale in *Moby-Dick* plays various roles to different characters. In Captain Ahab's obsessive, monomaniacal quest to kill it, the whale represents all evil, and Ahab believes it his duty and destiny to rid the world of it. Ishmael attempts through multiple scientific disciplines to understand the whale objectively, but fails—it is hidden underwater and mysterious to humans—reinforcing Melville's theme that humans can never know everything; here the whale represents the unknowable. Melville reverses white's usual connotation of purity in Ishmael's dread of white, associated with crashing waves, polar animals, albinos—all frightening and unnatural. White is often viewed as an absence of color, yet white light is the sum total of all colors in the spectrum. In the same way, white can signify both absence of meaning, and totality of meaning incomprehensible to humans. As a creature of nature, the whale also symbolizes how 19th-century white men's exploitative expansionistic actions were destroying the natural environment.

Reading
© Mometrix Media - flashcardsecrets.com/louisiana
English I

Explicate a few of the many ways F. Scott Fitzgerald used symbols to develop the theme of the American Dream's corruption by excessive wealth in *The Great Gatsby*. Include a comparison to an earlier great literary work.

Reading
© Mometrix Media - flashcardsecrets.com/louisiana
English I

Describe some ways in which Victor Hugo developed the theme of the importance of love and compassion in *Les Misérables*.

Reading
© Mometrix Media - flashcardsecrets.com/louisiana
English I

Explicate some of the ways Edgar Allan Poe develops the theme of paranoia and madness in his short story "The Tell-Tale Heart."

Reading
© Mometrix Media - flashcardsecrets.com/louisiana
English I

Explain a few ways that William Faulkner develops a theme of the past versus the future, or of preserving traditions against change, in his story "A Rose for Emily."

Reading
© Mometrix Media - flashcardsecrets.com/louisiana
English I

Describe some ways that Herman Melville developed a theme of humanity's finite knowledge through the symbol of the whale and the motif of whiteness in *Moby-Dick*; or, *The Whale*.

Reading
© Mometrix Media - flashcardsecrets.com/louisiana
English I

Discuss some of Ernest Hemingway's thematic development in his novella *The Old Man and the Sea*. Include how he reflects some themes from earlier literature.

In their attempts to persuade, writers often make mistakes in their thought processes and writing choices. These processes and choices are important to understand so you can make an informed decision about the author's credibility. Every author has a point of view, but authors demonstrate a **bias** when they ignore reasonable counterarguments or distort opposing viewpoints. A bias is evident whenever the author's claims are presented in a way that is unfair or inaccurate. Bias can be intentional or unintentional, but readers should be skeptical of the author's argument in either case. Remember that a biased author may still be correct. However, the author will be correct in spite of, not because of, his or her bias.

A **stereotype** is a bias applied specifically to a group of people or a place. Stereotyping is considered to be particularly abhorrent because it promotes negative, misleading generalizations about people. Readers should be very cautious of authors who use stereotypes in their writing. These faulty assumptions typically reveal the author's ignorance and lack of curiosity.

When you have an argumentative passage, you need to be sure that facts are presented to the reader from **reliable sources**. An opinion is what the author thinks about a given topic. An opinion is not common knowledge or proven by expert sources, instead the information is the personal beliefs and thoughts of the author. To distinguish between fact and opinion, a reader needs to consider the type of source that is presenting information, the information that backs-up a claim, and the author's motivation to have a certain point-of-view on a given topic. For example, if a panel of scientists has conducted multiple studies on the effectiveness of taking a certain vitamin, then the results are more likely to be factual than those of a company that is selling a vitamin and simply claims that taking the vitamin can produce positive effects. The company is motivated to sell their product, and the scientists are using the scientific method to prove a theory. Remember, if you find sentences that contain phrases such as "I think…", then the statement is an opinion.

The best literary analysis shows special insight into at least one important aspect of a text. When analyzing literary texts, it can be difficult to find a starting place. Many texts can be analyzed several different ways, often leaving an overwhelming number of options for writers to consider. However, narrowing the focus to a particular element of literature can be helpful when preparing to analyze a text. Symbolism, themes, and motifs are common starting points for literary analysis. These three methods of analysis can lead to a holistic analysis of a text, since they involve elements that are often distributed throughout the text. However, not all texts feature these elements in a way that facilitates a strong analysis, if they are present at all. It is also common to focus on character or plot development for analysis. These elements are compatible with theme, symbolism, and allusion. Setting and imagery, figurative language, and any external contexts can also contribute to analysis or complement one of these other elements. The application of a critical, or literary, theory to a text can also provide a thorough and strong analysis.

In works of prose such as novels, a group of connected sentences covering one main topic is termed a **paragraph**. In works of poetry, a group of verses similarly connected is called a **stanza**. In drama, when early works used verse, these were also divided into stanzas or **couplets**. Drama evolved to use predominantly prose. Overall, whether prose or verse, the conversation in a play is called **dialogue**. Large sections of dialogue spoken by one actor are called **soliloquies** or **monologues**. Dialogue that informs audiences but is unheard by other characters is called an **aside**. Novels and plays share certain common elements, such as **characters**, the people in the story; **plot**, the action of the story; **climax**, when action or dramatic tension reaches its highest point; and **denouement**, the resolution following the climax. Sections dividing novels are called **chapters**, while sections of plays are called **acts**. Subsections of plays' acts are called **scenes**. Novel chapters usually do not have subsections. However, some novels do include groups of chapters that form different sections.

In well-crafted literature, theme, structure, and plot are interdependent and inextricable: each element informs and reflects the others. The structure of a work is how it is organized. The theme is the central idea or meaning found in it. The plot is what happens in the story. Titles can also inform us of a work's theme. For instance, the title of Edgar Allan Poe's "The Tell-Tale Heart" informs readers of the story's theme of guilt before they even read about the repeated heartbeat the protagonist hears immediately before and constantly after committing and hiding a murder. Repetitive patterns of events or behaviors also give clues to themes. The same is true of symbols. For example, in F. Scott Fitzgerald's *The Great Gatsby,* for Jay Gatsby the green light at the end of the dock symbolizes Daisy Buchanan and his own dreams for the future. More generally, it is also understood as a symbol of the American Dream, and narrator Nick Carraway explicitly compares it to early settlers' sight of America rising from the ocean.

When we read parables, their themes are the lessons they aim to teach. When we read fables, the moral of each story is its theme. When we read fictional works, the authors' perspectives regarding life and human behavior are their themes. Unlike in parables and fables, themes in literary fiction are usually not meant to preach or teach the readers a lesson. Hence, themes in fiction are not as explicit as they are in parables or fables. Instead, they are implicit, and the reader only infers them. By analyzing the fictional characters through thinking about their actions and behavior, understanding the setting of the story, and reflecting on how its plot develops, the reader comes to infer the main theme of the work. When writers succeed, they communicate with their readers such that common ground is established between author and audience. While a reader's individual experience may differ in its details from the author's written story, both may share universal underlying truths which allow author and audience to connect.

Reading
© Mometrix Media - flashcardsecrets.com/louisiana
English I

Describe ways to distinguish between fact and opinion in an argumentative passage.

Reading
© Mometrix Media - flashcardsecrets.com/louisiana
English I

Discuss the identification of an author's biases and stereotypes.

Reading
© Mometrix Media - flashcardsecrets.com/louisiana
English I

Name, compare, and contrast some examples of correct terminology for various literary genres like poems, plays, and novels.

Reading
© Mometrix Media - flashcardsecrets.com/louisiana
English I

Describe strategies for approaching literary analysis and characteristics of strong literary analysis.

Reading
© Mometrix Media - flashcardsecrets.com/louisiana
English I

Discuss literary theme, its purpose, and how readers generally identify it.

Reading
© Mometrix Media - flashcardsecrets.com/louisiana
English I

Identify some ways in which readers of literature can discover what the main theme in a work is.

Authors can use **comparisons** like analogies, similes, and metaphors to persuade audiences. For example, a writer might represent excessive expenses as "hemorrhaging" money, which the author's recommended solution will stop. Authors can use negative word connotations to make some choices unappealing to readers, and positive word connotations to make others more appealing. Using **humor** can relax readers and garner their agreement. However, writers must take care: ridiculing opponents can be a successful strategy for appealing to readers who already agree with the author, but can backfire by angering other readers. **Rhetorical questions** need no answer, but create effect that can force agreement, such as asking the question, "Wouldn't you rather be paid more than less?" **Generalizations** persuade readers by being impossible to disagree with. Writers can easily make generalizations that appear to support their viewpoints, like saying, "We all want peace, not war" regarding more specific political arguments. **Transfer** and **association** persuade by example: if advertisements show attractive actors enjoying their products, audiences imagine they will experience the same. **Repetition** can also sometimes effectively persuade audiences.

To **appeal using reason**, writers present logical arguments, such as using "If... then... because" statements. To **appeal to emotions**, authors may ask readers how they would feel about something or to put themselves in another's place, present their argument as one that will make the audience feel good, or tell readers how they should feel. To **appeal to character**, **morality**, or **ethics**, authors present their points to readers as the right or most moral choices. Authors cite expert opinions to show readers that someone very knowledgeable about the subject or viewpoint agrees with the author's claims. **Testimonials**, usually via anecdotes or quotations regarding the author's subject, help build the audience's trust in an author's message through positive support from ordinary people. **Bandwagon appeals** claim that everybody else agrees with the author's argument and persuade readers to conform and agree, also. Authors **appeal to greed** by presenting their choice as cheaper, free, or more valuable for less cost. They **appeal to laziness** by presenting their views as more convenient, easy, or relaxing. Authors also anticipate potential objections and argue against them before audiences think of them, thereby depicting those objections as weak.

- An **anecdote** is a brief story authors may relate to their argument, which can illustrate their points in a more real and relatable way.
- **Aphorisms** concisely state common beliefs and may rhyme. For example, Benjamin Franklin's "Early to bed and early to rise / Makes a man healthy, wealthy, and wise" is an aphorism.
- **Allusions** refer to literary or historical figures to impart symbolism to a thing or person and to create reader resonance. In John Steinbeck's *Of Mice and Men,* protagonist George's last name is Milton. This alludes to John Milton, who wrote *Paradise Lost,* and symbolizes George's eventual loss of his dream.
- **Satire** exaggerates, ridicules, or pokes fun at human flaws or ideas, as in the works of Jonathan Swift and Mark Twain.
- A **parody** is a form of satire that imitates another work to ridicule its topic or style.
- A **paradox** is a statement that is true despite appearing contradictory.
- **Hyperbole** is overstatement using exaggerated language.
- An **oxymoron** combines seeming contradictions, such as "deafening silence."
- **Analogies** compare two things that share common elements.

In his *On Rhetoric,* ancient Greek philosopher Aristotle defined three basic types of appeal used in writing, which he called *pathos, ethos,* and *logos.* **Pathos** means suffering or experience and refers to appeals to the emotions (the English word *pathetic* comes from this root). Writing that is meant to entertain audiences, by making them either happy, as with comedy, or sad, as with tragedy, uses *pathos.* Aristotle's *Poetics* states that evoking the emotions of terror and pity is one of the criteria for writing tragedy. **Ethos** means character and connotes ideology (the English word *ethics* comes from this root). Writing that appeals to credibility, based on academic, professional, or personal merit, uses *ethos.* **Logos** means "I say" and refers to a plea, opinion, expectation, word or speech, account, opinion, or reason (the English word *logic* comes from this root.) Aristotle used it to mean persuasion that appeals to the audience through reasoning and logic to influence their opinions.

Critical thinking skills are mastered through understanding various types of writing and the different purposes authors can have for writing different passages. Every author writes for a purpose. When you understand their purpose and how they accomplish their goal, you will be able to analyze their writing and determine whether or not you agree with their conclusions.

Readers must always be aware of the difference between fact and opinion. A **fact** can be subjected to analysis and proven to be true. An **opinion**, on the other hand, is the author's personal thoughts or feelings and may not be altered by research or evidence. If the author writes that the distance from New York City to Boston is about two hundred miles, then he or she is stating a fact. If the author writes that New York City is too crowded, then he or she is giving an opinion because there is no objective standard for overpopulation. Opinions are often supported by facts. For instance, an author might use a comparison between the population density of New York City and that of other major American cities as evidence of an overcrowded population. An opinion supported by facts tends to be more convincing. On the other hand, when authors support their opinions with other opinions, readers should employ critical thinking and approach the argument with skepticism.

- **Similes** (stated comparisons using the words *like* or *as*) and **metaphors** (stated comparisons that do not use *like* or *as*) are considered forms of analogy.
- When using logic to reason with audiences, **syllogism** refers either to deductive reasoning or a deceptive, very sophisticated, or subtle argument.
- **Deductive reasoning** moves from general to specific, **inductive reasoning** from specific to general.
- **Diction** is author word choice that establishes tone and effect.
- **Understatement** achieves effects like contrast or irony by downplaying or describing something more subtly than warranted.
- **Chiasmus** uses parallel clauses, the second reversing the order of the first. Examples include T. S. Eliot's "Has the Church failed mankind, or has mankind failed the Church?" and John F. Kennedy's "Ask not what your country can do for you; ask what you can do for your country."
- **Anaphora** regularly repeats a word or phrase at the beginnings of consecutive clauses or phrases to add emphasis to an idea. A classic example of anaphora was Winston Churchill's emphasis of determination: "We shall fight in the trenches. We shall fight on the oceans. We shall fight in the sky."

Reading
© Mometrix Media - flashcardsecrets.com/louisiana
English I

Explain several persuasive techniques that informational text authors use to get readers to agree with their points.

Reading
© Mometrix Media - flashcardsecrets.com/louisiana
English I

Describe several methods of persuasion that writers of informational text can use to convince readers of their viewpoints.

Reading
© Mometrix Media - flashcardsecrets.com/louisiana
English I

Identify the three kinds of classical author appeals and their source. Define each one.

Reading
© Mometrix Media - flashcardsecrets.com/louisiana
English I

Name several rhetorical devices that informational text authors can use to communicate their perspectives and achieve their purposes with readers most effectively. Include brief definitions of each and examples of some.

Reading
© Mometrix Media - flashcardsecrets.com/louisiana
English I

Identify and briefly define a number of rhetorical strategies that authors may use in informational texts to convey their messages better to readers. Give examples of two of these.

Reading
© Mometrix Media - flashcardsecrets.com/louisiana
English I

Discuss facts and opinions.

Thank you for purchasing Mometrix flashcards!

We have painstakingly reviewed piles of content and boiled it all down to the most critical information most likely to be on the exam. Your diligent use of these flashcards will help you get the results you want.

As you start reviewing these flashcards, it may seem a bit overwhelming at first. We have intentionally packed each flashcard with a lot of information to completely cover the critical concepts over which your test questions are based. Test makers intentionally try to trip you up by the way they word the questions. The reason they do this is to make sure the test-taker truly understands the information and didn't just memorize it. We have designed these flashcards to help you get the answers right, regardless of how the questions are worded on the test.

How to Access Your Online Resources

For your convenience, we have made your online resources accessible at:
mometrix.com/resources719/laenglishiflash

The Leitner Method of Studying Flashcards: Maximum Learning in Minimum Time

In the 1970's, a German psychologist named Sebastian Leitner developed a "learning machine" using flashcards that can supercharge your success by using the power of prioritization and positive feedback. This approach to using flashcards maximizes your time and makes studying more like a game.

Visit the online resources page to see a video demonstrating the Leitner study method!

Here's how his system works: Start by having three separate folders or boxes, the first labeled **Every Day**, the second labeled **Tuesday & Thursday**, and the third labeled **Friday**. The labels tell you which days you should look at the cards in each box. As you go through the flashcard deck for the first time on Monday, place any cards you answer correctly into the **Tuesday & Thursday** box. Study any you miss as you go through the cards, but any that you miss have to go back into the **Every Day** box. On Tuesday, you'll study the cards in both of the first two boxes, moving any you miss back to the first box and any you answer correctly to the third box. Your goal is to get all of the cards into the third box and keep them there!

Copyright © 2026 by Mometrix Media LLC. All rights reserved.
Written and edited by the Mometrix Exam Secrets Test Prep Team
Printed in the United States of America

Mometrix **TEST PREPARATION**

ProductID: LAEnglishIFlash

Louisiana
English I EOC

Flashcard Study System

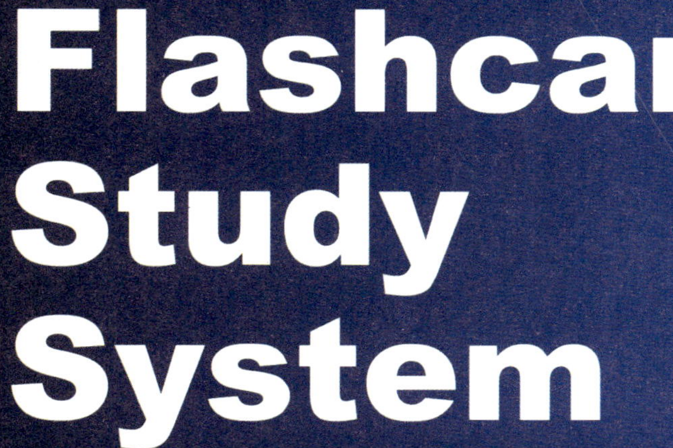

Mometrix
TEST PREPARATION

ISBN: 978-1-5167-1939-6

9 781516 719396

Easy-to-separate, perforated flashcards enclosed.

Mometrix Test Preparation is not affiliated with or endorsed by any official testing organization. All organizational and test names are trademarks of their respective owners.